DISCOVERING
OUR HERITAGE

SAUDI ARABIA

A DESERT KINGDOM

BY KEVIN M. MCCARTHY

DILLON PRESS

PARSIPPANY, NEW JERSEY

Acknowledgments

Photo Credits

(Photo credits from previous edition.)

The photographs are reproduced through the courtesy of the following people and agencies: Hans Christian Heap; Moodie R. Khaldi; Anas Abu Mansour; Kevin M. McCarthy; the Saudi Arabian Ministry of Information; UNICEF; the Imperial War Museum, London; the U.S. Department of the Navy; Michael Evans/the White House; and Historical Pictures Service (p. 106).

(Second edition photo credits.)

Front Cover: Photos, the Saudi Arabian Ministry of Information. Map, Ortelius Design.

Liaison International/© Diana Walker: 116. Kevin McCarthy: 13, 69, 102. Photo Researchers, Inc./© Allen Green: 23. SBG: 5. Map, Ortelius Design: 6.

Every effort has been made to locate the original sources. If any errors or omissions have occurred, corrections will be made.

Library of Congress Cataloging-in-Publication Data

McCarthy, Kevin.
    Saudi Arabia: a desert kingdom/by Kevin McCarthy.—2nd ed.
        p. cm.—(Discovering our heritage)
    Includes bibliographical references (p.) and index.
    Summary: Examines the religious, family-oriented, traditional society of modern Saudi Arabia, its transition from poor to rich nation, and its relationship with America. Appendixes present the Arabic alphabet and list consulates and embassies in the United States and Canada.
    ISBN 0-382-39608-1 (LSB)
    1. Saudi Arabia—Juvenile literature. [1. Saudi Arabia.]
I. Title. II. Series.
DS204.M33 1997   96-14962
953.8—dc20

Copyright © 1997 by Kevin M. McCarthy

Cover and book design By Michelle Farinella

Published by Dillon Press
A Division of Simon & Schuster
299 Jefferson Road, Parsippany, NJ 07054

Second Edition
Printed in the United States of America
10 9 8 7 6 5 4 3 2 1

CONTENTS

Fast Facts About Saudi Arabia 4

Map of Saudi Arabia 6

1 A Kingdom in the Desert 7

2 The Islamic Life 21

3 Sand and Oil 33

4 The Spoken Story 49

5 Festivals and Foods 59

6 Family 71

7 Schools for the Future 83

8 Racing on Camels, Hunting With Birds 92

9 The Arab World in the United States 104

Appendix A: Saudi Arabian Consulates and

     Embassies in the United States and Canada 119

Appendix B: Arabic Symbols 120

Glossary 122

Selected Bibliography .125

Index 126

FAST FACTS ABOUT SAUDI ARABIA

Official Name: *Al-Mamlaka Al Arabiyya Al-Saudiyya*

Capital: Riyadh

Location: The Arabian Peninsula, the piece of land between Africa and Asia in the Middle East.

Area: 830,000 square miles (2,149,690 square kilometers); it stretches about 1,145 miles (1,843 kilometers) north to south and about 1,290 miles (2,076 kilometers) east to west; it has 1,515 miles (2,438 kilometers) of coastline, three-quarters of that on the Red Sea and one-quarter on the Arabian (Persian) Gulf. The country is about one-third the size of the continental United States and occupies about four-fifths the area of the Arabian Peninsula.

Elevation: *Highest*—10,279 feet (3,133 kilometers) in the Asir Mountains; *Lowest*—Sea level.

Population: Estimated 1995 population—17,608,000; about 21 persons per square mile (8 persons per square kilometer); *Distribution*—80 percent live in cities and towns; 20 percent, in rural areas.

Form of Government: Monarchy. *Head of government*—King

Some Important Products: Petroleum; fertilizer, concrete; oranges, rice, wheat, vegetables; goats, camels.

Basic Unit of Money: Riyal

Language: Arabic

Religion: Islam

Flag: A green background with the Arabic words for "There is no God but Allah and Muhammad is His Prophet" and a sword in white.

Emblem: Saudi Arabia's coat of arms shows a date palm above two crossed swords. The palm tree represents vitality and growth; the swords symbolize justice and strength rooted in faith.

Restrictions: Forbidden items include alcohol, narcotics, weapons, ammunition, pork, and pornography. Visitors must be able to document their prescription drugs. Only persons of the Islamic faith are allowed to enter Mecca (Makkah) and Medina (Madinah).

National Anthem: "Al-Salaam Al-Malaki Al-Saudi" ("Royal Anthem of Saudi Arabia")

Some Major Holidays: Id al-Adha (the date varies); Id al-Fitr (following the Islamic month of Ramadan); National Day, September 23.

Official Saudi Home Page: http://imedl.saudi.net This home page from the Royal Embassy of Saudi Arabia will provide more information about the country, its monthly newsletter, and its quarterly magazine, *Saudi Arabia*.

A KINGDOM IN THE DESERT

Whenever we ride in a car, listen to a CD, or drink from a plastic cup, chances are we're using a product whose raw material, oil, comes from a country many thousands of miles away from us: the Kingdom of Saudi Arabia. It's a country that we depend on in many different ways but one that many of us know very little about.

If you were asked to list some things that the name *Saudi Arabia* brings to your mind, you might write down oil wells, camels, or huge deserts. You might mention a white-robed Arab, sword hanging from his rope belt, dashing across a sand dune on an Arabian stallion, ready to do battle. Saudi Arabia does have oil wells and camels and huge deserts. But today you probably wouldn't find many white-robed Arabs dashing across sand dunes on stallions. Pickup trucks have replaced horses in many cities and towns and there are roads across the desert, too.

This huge country lies at the southwestern edge of Asia, next to Africa and near the eastern end of the Mediterranean Sea. The body of land on which Saudi Arabia is located is the Arabian Peninsula. It takes up as much space as the part of the United States that lies east of the Mississippi River. If you look at a map of the area,

you'll notice the Red Sea along the west coast of Saudi Arabia. It's not really a body of red water. In fact, it's usually blue-green in color, but sometimes it turns reddish-brown when plants in it called algae die off. It also has some red coral that the world has long valued when carved into jewelry or other decorations.

The mountains of the Asir and Hejaz regions hug the coast along the Red Sea and manage to catch most of the rain from the clouds passing east over the country. That means the rest of Saudi Arabia is very, very dry—one of the driest countries on earth. Sometimes there is no rain in the central part of Saudi Arabia for several years at a time.

The eastern coast of Saudi Arabia stretches along one of the most important waterways of the world—the Arabian, or Persian, Gulf. This area, with its oil rigs in the gulf or on the desert, supplies many nations with much-needed oil. Scientists estimate that about one-fourth of all the oil in the world lies under Saudi Arabia. That's a lot of oil!

Some of the countries that border Saudi Arabia—such as Jordan, Iraq, and Kuwait—may have names familiar to you. Names of other border countries—Yemen, Qatar, Oman, Bahrain, and the United Arab Emirates—may be unfamiliar. Because the vast stretches of desert have few solid features by which to mark borders, Saudi Arabia and some of its neighbors have set up neutral zones instead of

*In Saudi Arabia's vast deserts, the wind often shifts
the huge sand dunes.*

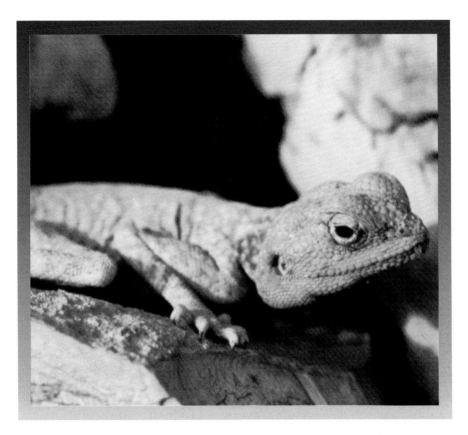

A desert lizard whose head turns blue when it senses danger

having borders. They share the mineral wealth they find in those zones.

In the southern part of the country lies the world's largest sand desert, the *Rub al Khali*, a name that means "the Empty Quarter." Very few people live in that desolate area, which is about the size of Texas, and you would search long and hard before you found any animals, either. Most people, animals, and plants could not survive for long in that very hot desert.

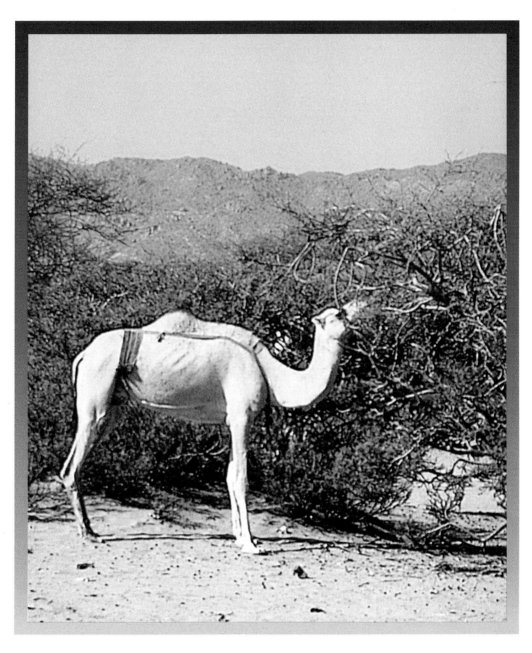

Camels can live very well in the desert because they can go for long periods without water.

*Precious water is piped to dry areas, permitting
the desert to be farmed.*

Getting Water

Most of Saudi Arabia, in fact, consists of deserts: dry, sandy areas. The few river beds remain dry most of the year. When it does rain—and this isn't often—the water rushes down the river beds and quickly disappears into the sandy soil. People value water so highly in this dry land that water costs more than gasoline! The Saudis use their supply of water very carefully. When they wash their cars, for example, they use as little water as possible.

Many Saudi Arabian cities get fresh, drinkable water from the sea. Large processing plants heat sea water and

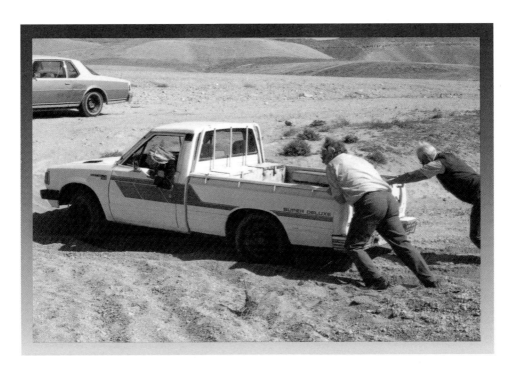

The deep desert sand can trap the wheels of trucks.

turn it to steam; when that happens, the salt separates from the vapor. The salty leftover water is pumped away; the steam is cooled and turned into water. This process is called desalination. Sometimes this process can work too well. Then some salt must be put back so the water has a better taste. Once the water is ready, it is pumped hundreds of miles through pipelines to cities throughout the kingdom.

While it's true that most of Saudi Arabia consists of deserts, there are scattered oases in the deserts. There, palm trees, green plants, and bright flowers grow—all fed from underground streams. People settled around these fertile spots to raise crops and tend herds of animals.

In the past, an oasis was a welcome sight to caravans of travelers on camels winding their way across the harsh desert. Even today, travelers driving along the wide-open highways look for places to picnic or to have just a cup of tea in the cool oases along the roads.

Two Treasures

At times it's hard to imagine that beneath the miles and miles of sand dunes lies something of immense value: oil. Saudi Arabia supplies many nations with this much-needed product. The valuable mineral has helped the country change from being very, very poor to being very, very rich.

But it is also rich in something besides oil. For the 900 million people around the world who follow the religion of Islam—people whom we call Muslims—Saudi Arabia has a treasure far more important. It has the holy cities of Mecca (or Makkah) and Medina (or Madinah) near the west coast. In those cities some 1,400 years ago, a holy man named Muhammad founded Islam, one of the world's major religions. Five times a day, seven days a week, the world's Muslims face toward Mecca, no matter how far away they are, and say their prayers.

Every Muslim tries to travel to Mecca at least once in order to make a pilgrimage, which is a journey to a shrine or sacred place. In the past, these pilgrims had to cross the

Pilgrims arrive by plane in Jidda and then make their way to the holy cities of Mecca and Medina.

desert, sometimes in the heat of the summer, to get to Mecca. They had to travel by ship or camel or horse for many weeks. Today, pilgrims can fly from their faraway countries by the most modern jets or drive on superhighways in air-conditioned cars and buses. Each year over a million Muslims journey to Mecca from all over the globe to fulfill their goal of praying in that holy place.

Mecca and Medina are unusual in that you must be a Muslim to enter them. Security police on the outskirts of each city check the identification papers of all incoming visitors. They make sure only Muslims enter the cities.

Nearby, on the Red Sea, lies the beautiful city of Jidda, called by many "the bride of the Red Sea." It is an old city, so old in fact that many people believe that Eve, the first woman and the wife of Adam, is buried there. For years Jidda has been the main port and business center for Saudi Arabia. It is also the place where the million or so pilgrims arrive each year before making their way to Mecca and Medina. From the time the Suez Canal, at the top of the Red Sea, was opened in 1869, thousands of ships have passed from Asia and East Africa to Jidda, through the canal, and on to the Mediterranean Sea and Europe.

Like many places in Saudi Arabia, Jidda's main problem for many years was a lack of fresh water. Up until the 1920s, the city had just a single tree. Since that time, Jidda has found new sources of water and has planted many trees and flowers. Along its miles of waterfront, the city has constructed beautiful monuments and many picnic benches. Families love to go there during cool evenings and on weekends throughout the year to picnic, wade in the warm water of the Red Sea, and meet their friends.

The Oil Cities

Saudi Arabia produces more oil than any other country. Over on the east coast, along the Arabian, or Persian, Gulf, lie the oil cities of Ad Dammam and

Dhahran. These neighboring cities are host to thousands of oil workers, from many different countries, who bring out the rich mineral from beneath the sands and sea. From these ports the oil is sent on its way to countries around the world.

The Arabian American Oil Company—Aramco for short—does most of the oil work in the area. For its many workers, it provides housing in small towns resembling oil towns in Kansas and Texas. With swimming pools, bowling alleys, and stores, the towns are in sharp contrast with the surrounding desert and the nearby Arab towns.

Aramco was once owned and operated by U.S. businesses. Beginning in the 1970s, Saudi Arabia took more and more control of Aramco. Today it owns the company and makes the decisions about how much oil to pump out of the ground. The company is now called Saudi Aramco.

Saudi Arabia belongs to the Organization of Petroleum Exporting Countries (OPEC). This group of countries sets the price of their oil and thus has a major influence on the price of gasoline at your local gas station. Understandably, OPEC and the rest of the world look on the Ad Dammam area as a place very important to the whole oil industry.

The Garden Capital

The capital city of Riyadh lies between Jidda and Ad Dammam, in the middle of a large stretch of desert. The

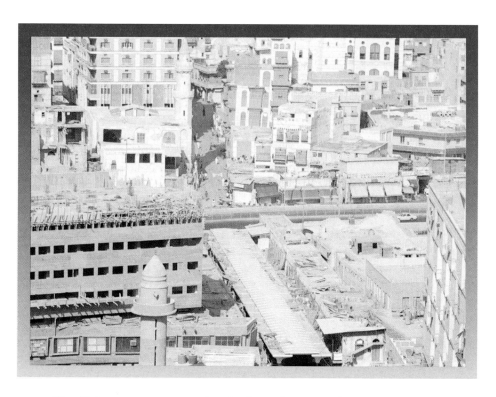

Riyadh has grown tremendously from the time when it was a small city with mud buildings.

name *Riyadh* means "the Gardens": there is an oasis at this spot, fed by underground streams. In the early 1950s, Riyadh had only mud houses and clay palaces, but oil wealth has changed all that. The once-small town has become a booming city, with many palaces, government buildings, schools, and large homes. Over one million people live in and around the city, and its airport, King Khalid International Airport, is the largest in the world.

From time to time, sandstorms remind the inhabitants of Riyadh that desert surrounds the city. And the intense summer heat of June, July, and August usually keeps everyone indoors during the day in the coolness of air-conditioned homes and offices. But because Riyadh lies between both coasts, and between the port of Jidda and the oil fields near Ad Dammam, it has become the center for government.

The rulers of the country spend much of their time in Riyadh. These rulers include a king and many princes, all from the same family, the Al Saud family. The king and princes are Muslim, as are the Saudi people.

The king and senior members of the royal family rule the country. There is no legislature or congress. Instead, the laws of Islam are the laws of the country. Religious leaders also help to run the country.

The Saudi king differs from most kings in that citizens of the country can see him in once-a-week meetings that are open to the people. They can talk with him during these sessions, ask him for help with a particular problem, give him their opinion about something, or just complain.

For example, someone might need help in settling an argument with a neighbor or in going to school in another country or in starting a business. Imagine being able to talk to the head of your country about such things!

More than 17 million people live in Saudi Arabia, but, fortunately, most of the people don't have to see the king very often. They can also visit their local mayor or governor any week to discuss their problems.

The people who live in Saudi Arabia are called Saudis. Most Saudis are Arabs, a people tan-skinned from years in the sun. The fiercely proud people of this area lived for centuries cut off from the world. For many years the rest of the world, except the thousands of Muslims who made their annual pilgrimages to the holy places of Islam, paid almost no attention to the Arabian Peninsula. But since the discovery of oil in Saudi Arabia in the 1930s all that has changed. Now, businesspeople and others with something to sell flock to Riyadh and Jidda trying to convince the Saudis to buy from them. The world became even more aware of the country's importance during the 1990–1991 Gulf War, when Iraq attacked Kuwait. Troops from Western nations and Arab nations joined Saudi defense forces to liberate Kuwait and restore order to the region. The world has finally taken note of Saudi Arabia, and wants to know more about the people of this nation.

THE ISLAMIC LIFE

To understand a Saudi Arabian, we must know something about the religion of Islam. Islam governs all the actions of Saudis and guides them from birth, through life, to death. For most people of Saudi Arabia, Islam provides guidelines and rules about what to do and what not to do. Even a first-time visitor to Saudi Arabia can see just how great a role Islam plays. Five times a day, every day of the week, the call to prayer interrupts the silence or noise of every Saudi town and city.

From high atop the minaret, or tower, near each mosque comes a call in Arabic: "God is most great." When Muslims hear these words, they stop what they are doing, face in the direction of the holy city of Mecca, and lift their thoughts to God. Shopkeepers close and lock their doors, schoolteachers lead their students to prayer rooms, and broadcasters interrupt television programs to announce the start of prayer time. The whole nation pauses and turns its thoughts to God. This happens throughout the day: at dawn, at noon, in midafternoon, at sunset, and after dark.

If prayer time finds a Saudi family out driving or having a picnic in the desert, the family will stop and say their prayers. This frequent praying may be surprising to many people in the United States and other Western

No matter where they are in Saudi Arabia, Muslims stop to pray five times a day.

countries who usually go to their churches or synagogues just once a week.

Men usually pray in the mosques; women prefer the privacy of their homes. Women can use the mosques, but most of them find it more convenient to say their prayers at home. (Since most Saudi women don't work outside the home, they spend most of the day in their own dwellings.) At least one mosque is found in every village, town, and city. In large cities, such as Riyadh and Jidda, you can find a mosque every few blocks, always within easy walking distance.

If you were to pass by a mosque during prayer time, you would see hundreds of shoes outside the main doors.

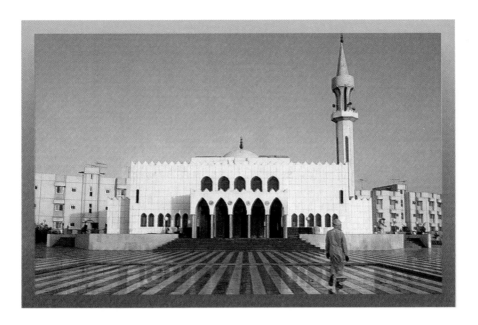

The slender minaret of this mosque in Jidda stands tall against the sky.

This is because the worshippers remove their shoes before washing their hands, faces, and feet. Then they kneel on the beautiful rugs in the mosque as they make their bows to Mecca. In this way the rugs remain clean for everyone.

An Honest Nation

As a result of their powerful belief in God, the Saudis are honest in a way that people of few other countries are. In Saudi Arabia, you seldom hear of crime—acts such as murder, theft, smuggling, or bribery. In fact, if you mistakenly leave something behind in a shop, you can return several days later and find that the shopkeeper has kept your package safe for you.

You may have heard that the Saudis cut off the head of a convicted murderer or chop off the hand of a thief. This is true, but these punishments seldom happen, since criminals avoid Saudi Arabia. The Saudis have these harsh punishments because that is what the Islamic religion tells them to do. The knowledge of these punishments makes the country quite safe for everyone. Anyone can walk the streets of Saudi cities late at night without fear of attack.

Even the Saudi flag reminds the people of their religion, since it shows the Arabic words meaning "There is no God but Allah and Muhammad is His prophet." (The word *prophet* refers to a holy person whom God uses to speak to the people of the world.) The green color in the flag stands for prosperity, and the white color stands for peace. The sword is a symbol of justice and strength. Because the Saudi flag flies throughout Saudi Arabia, it reminds everyone of how religious that nation strives to be.

Islam means "submission to God's will" and *Muslim* means "one who submits." Muslims worship one God, Allah. They believe that God told certain truths to the prophet Muhammad of Mecca, through the angel Gabriel, and gave him principles by which the people of the world should live. Their holy book, called the Qur'an, or Koran, contains these truths and principles.

Islam began in the seventh century, about A.D. 610. The people in Mecca did not at first appreciate the teachings of Muhammad and forced him and his followers to flee to the nearby city of Medina. That flight in A.D. 622 is known as the Hijrah, and the date marks the starting point of the Muslim calendar.

The Muslim calendar differs from the Gregorian calendar, the one we use in the West. Though the Islamic year has twelve months, like ours, the months have about twenty-nine days, unlike ours, which usually have thirty or thirty-one days. Their year, then, is eleven days shorter than the Western, or Gregorian, year. The year 1997 on our calendar is known as 1418 on the Islamic calendar. The Saudis also tell time differently. They officially start their day at sunset, not at twelve midnight the way we do in the United States. You can buy watches in Saudi Arabia that have two faces, one that shows Western time and the other that shows Islamic time.

The Spirit of Generosity

Saudi Arabia is different from the West in other ways—for example, in taxes. The government there, unlike governments in most of the world today, does not collect taxes. It doesn't have to, since it earns so much money from its oil. How much money? Well, in the early 1980s the country was earning over $100 million every day. Today the country continues to earn a great deal of money from oil, but the amount of money fluctuates, goes up or down, depending on the price of oil. As long as the world continues to run on oil, that money will keep coming in.

But that doesn't mean the Saudis keep all that money for themselves. Because so many of the people are deeply religious, they give much of their money away, in alms, or gifts, to help the world's poor people and those struck by disaster. If an earthquake or tidal wave, for instance, strikes a country, especially one nearby Saudi Arabia or another Muslim country, the Saudis will often rush in supplies to help the affected towns and villages.

The Arabs of Saudi Arabia have several sayings or proverbs that tell us much about their attitudes about money. For example, they say "A rich miser is poorer than a poor man" and "A heart free from care is better than a full purse."

This attitude about money is shown by everyone, from high government officials to shopkeepers, as is a trust of others. For example, recently a woman went into a clothing store in Riyadh to look for some dresses. After she chose a particularly pretty dress, she realized that she hadn't brought any money with her. The shopkeeper looked at her, judged her to be honest, and told her, "Don't worry about it. Take the dress home, try it out, and—if you like it—bring in the money next week." He didn't even ask for her name or address.

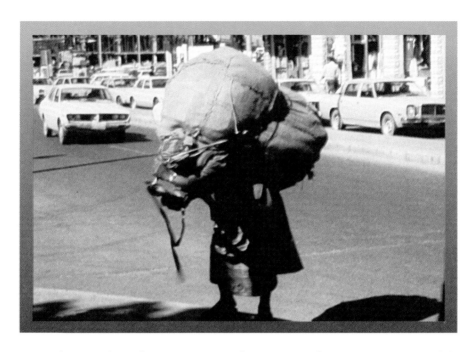

Workers such as this porter come from many other countries to work in Saudi Arabia.

Saudis also bring in workers from many different nations for help in building hospitals and schools, setting up telephone lines, and constructing highways through the desert. On any day, especially in the big cities of Riyadh and Jidda, you can see workers from Korea, Pakistan, Turkey, Germany, England, or the United States. Those workers earn good salaries, much of which they may send back home to their families. In this way Saudi Arabian wealth spreads to many peoples of the world. In return, those workers help the Saudis to build modern schools and great ports for ships and to keep the streets as clean as they can. Teachers from many different lands are training Saudi students to become doctors, nurses, and computer programmers—whatever the country needs to get ready for the twenty-first century.

The People of the Desert

Most Saudis live in cities or towns and have businesses or farms, like many other peoples of the world. But some Saudis—the wandering herders called Bedouins— have changed their way of life very little in the last thousand years.

Those Bedouins who still live in the desert ride their horses and camels while they herd their sheep and other animals from place to place. You can sometimes see the large black tents of these people far off in the desert. Families might be resting in the shade of these goat-hair tents from the heat of the noonday sun or preparing their midafternoon meal. Perhaps the father is telling his children, all gathered around him, about Arab warriors and leaders from the past. Perhaps he is instructing them on how to survive in the harsh desert.

In the summer, when the temperature can reach 120 degrees Fahrenheit, Bedouins will usually camp near freshwater wells. Even if the water in the wells looks dirty or smells bad, the camels don't seem to mind, and they drink their fill. However, Bedouins sometimes go for

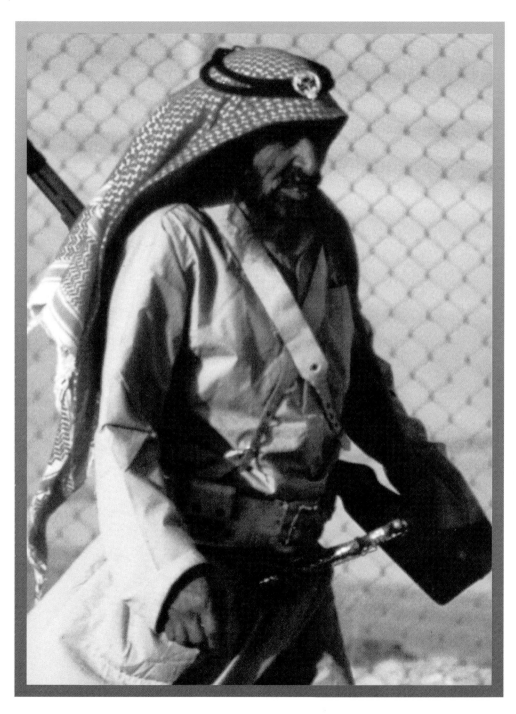

Bedouin men have the reputation of being hospitable to friends and guests but fierce to enemies.

Bedouin women are said to be very private people, and they are seldom seen by outsiders who visit their camps.

several months without drinking water; instead, they milk their camels and live on camel milk.

If a stranger shows up in their camp, the Bedouins there usually make that person feel at home as much as possible. They offer the visitor whatever food they have, including delicious dates and coffee. They may even kill one of their sheep or goats to provide a good meal for the stranger. The Bedouins are a sturdy people, as the hard life of the desert demands, but they can be extremely kind and hospitable.

The women of the family usually stay in the background during a stranger's visit. They prepare the meal but won't join the others in the eating of it. Bedouin women guard their privacy, wearing black veils and floor-length robes, called abas, that cover their whole bodies from head to feet. The laws of Islam require women to dress in this modest way. Sometimes the veils have little slits that allow the women to peer out. It is considered impolite for strangers to stare at the women or talk to them.

The Bedouins have certain rules of conduct that they follow, even in war. For example, if they fought a battle with a neighboring tribe, they would not hurt the women or children of the other tribe. And if they found something along a caravan trail, something that another traveler had lost, they would leave it right where they found it. When the traveler who had lost it returned to look for it, the object would be right where it was lost.

The evenings on the desert may be passed by storytelling or even singing songs. There are no radios or televisions, so those wandering shepherds and their families go to sleep under the stars when it gets dark and then wake up at dawn.

Life in the desert can be very difficult. The desert people have to be careful to avoid animals such as scorpions, snakes, and wolves. From time to time, they may see a fox or a baboon, but such animals usually stay away from people. Occasionally, a dreadful sandstorm will come up, blocking out the sun and making life miserable. Sometimes the storm goes on for several days. The sand swirls around at high speed, getting into everything, even the noses and mouths of well-protected travelers.

That's when the long headcoverings of the Saudis come in handy. The men can wrap the cloths around their faces as shields against the stinging wind. What a welcome relief it is when the wind and sand die down once again, the sun comes out, and life returns to normal.

Whether they live in city houses or goat-hair tents, Saudis have their strong Islamic faith and spirit of generosity in common. They are a tough, proud people who have made a place for themselves in the desert.

SAND AND OIL

The modern nation of Saudi Arabia traces its beginnings to a dark night in 1902. A twenty-one-year-old man lay in wait for a local ruler to come out of his fort for his morning tasks. The young man, whose name was Abdulaziz Al Saud, had led a small group of loyal followers across the huge desert from the nearby country of Kuwait. He was determined to capture the city of Riyadh for his family.

Abdulaziz belonged to the Al Saud family; the local ruler he awaited belonged to the Al Rashid family. These two rival Arab families had fought for many years to control the towns and cities of the Arabian Peninsula. Throughout history, people in many parts of the world have made war on other people because of religion, water, land, or even different skin color. In Saudi Arabia the dividing line was a person's tribe or family. Abdulaziz knew this well and was determined to restore to his tribe and family the control of the country.

When the local ruler came out of his fort that morning, Abdulaziz jumped up from his hiding place, yelled out a challenge, ran across to the fort, and tackled his enemy. He then leaped to his feet, killed the ruler with his sword, and took control of the fort. Thus began the rule of the Al Saud family, a close-knit group that gave its name and many members of its family to Saudi Arabia. The family would guide the nation into modern times.

Ancient Peoples

For most of its earlier history, though, Saudi Arabia had not had a single family ruling it. Thousands of years ago, during the ancient Ice Age—when snow and ice covered Europe and Asia—the Arabian Peninsula had rich grasslands and flowing streams. As the climate of the world slowly changed, the land there became dry and unfit for most people.

The rest of the world knew this land as the home of hardy people who wandered with their animal herds from oasis to oasis. An occasional caravan of traders from Africa or Asia would crisscross its way over the vast deserts, carrying perfumes such as frankincense and myrrh to many countries. Ports grew up along the coast, but their city dwellers had little contact with the desert peoples inland.

The great empire builders of the Middle East—such as the Babylonians, the Assyrians, and the Persians—went around the Arabian Peninsula rather than across it, since the land seemed so desolate and poor. However, one group of people, the Nabateans, decided to stay.

During the three hundred years before and one hundred years after the birth of Christ, the Nabateans lived in the northwestern part of Saudi Arabia, along one of the major caravan routes. These people learned to build dams in riverbeds, collect water in large tanks, and irrigate their fields. They also built large tombs in the rocks, over a hundred of which still stand as reminders of Nabateans' great skill.

The Nabateans taxed the caravans that carried spices up and down the Red Sea coast along the inland route near these tombs. When the Romans began using ships to trade spices up and down the Red Sea, this inland spice route lost its importance. It was then that the Nabateans left the area and moved to another country.

Muhammad and Islam

The most important period in the history of the Arabian Peninsula was the time between A.D. 571 and 632. In this period, the prophet Muhammad was born, grew up, founded Islam, and died. One hundred years later, his followers rode out of Arabia on swift horses to conquer much of the known world, including Egypt, North Africa, Spain, Syria, Persia, Afghanistan, and Central Asia.

Because most of the conquered lands were to the east of Arabia, the Caliph, or the head of Islam, eventually

moved to Damascus in Syria. There he was closer to the center of the Islamic territory and could govern more easily.

Although thousands of pilgrims still went to Mecca and Medina, the holy cities, the Arabian Peninsula was no longer the center of Islam. Ships and caravans came less frequently. Since there was no strong central government located in the country, Arabian tribes fought one another. For hundreds of years this tribal warfare would continue.

In the 1500s, the Turks of the Ottoman Empire conquered Egypt and Syria and also took control of the Arabian Peninsula. They would control Arabia—sometimes strictly—until the time of World War I, in the early 1900s. The Turkish headquarters were in Constantinople (Istanbul), Turkey. Since the Turkish rulers were far away, they mostly ignored the many tribal wars going on in the Arabian Peninsula.

The Great Reformer

During this time of tribal warfare, some of the tribes stopped following the strict rules of Islam. They did not perform all the duties of Islam, and some even worshipped other, older gods. In the 1700s, a man named Muhammad ibn Abd Al Wahhab began a movement to stop this. He told these tribes that they were wrong to forget their religious duties, and by doing so he made enemies. But many people did listen to Al Wahhab's message.

The ancient Nabatean people left behind huge tombs carved into the rocks in the desert.

Al Wahhab finally joined forces with a strong tribe, the House of Saud. Together, the Wahhab and Saudi warriors had a mission—to bring Arabs back to the correct practice of Islam. They began to take over many towns in western Arabia.

When these forces took control of the holy cities of Mecca and Medina in 1802, the Ottoman Turks could no longer ignore what was going on. They asked one of their best generals, Mehemet Ali, to put down these Arabs as soon as possible. Ali sent two of his sons with large armies. At first, their modern weapons, though better than those of their enemies, were no match for the hit-and-run desert tactics of the Arabs. In the end, however, the Turks defeated the tribes and destroyed some of their towns.

Even after this defeat, the Arabs of the peninsula wanted to be rid of their Turkish government. In 1916, the Arabs of the west coast joined forces with an unusual Westerner—the British soldier T. E. Lawrence, better known as Lawrence of Arabia. With his assistance, the Arabs harassed the Turks by attacking the Turks' forts and blowing up the famous Hejaz Railway, built to take pilgrims to the city of Medina. The Turks eventually left Arabia for good, abandoning the desert land in which they had found it hard to live and fight.

The way was then clear for young Abdulaziz Al Saud to take over the Arabian Peninsula. After he captured

T. E. Lawrence, called Lawrence of Arabia, was a British soldier who helped the Arabs overthrow their Turkish rulers.

Riyadh in 1902, he spent the next twenty-five years conquering other tribes in the country. To make peace with some tribes, and because he realized how important large families were, he often married the daughter or widow of a local tribal leader. (Islam allows a man to have up to four wives at a time.) Often there were children from these marriages. In the end, Abdulaziz had more than forty sons and countless daughters. From these children would come the rulers of modern Saudi Arabia.

The New Kingdom

On September 18, 1932, the Kingdom of Saudi Arabia was officially formed. Most of the world, however, paid little attention to what was going on in that region. What was that place, they thought, except miles and miles of desert? The new nation was so poor that the person in charge of finances, the minister of the treasury, at one time kept the nation's money in a box under his bed.

All this began to change, of course, when oil was struck in 1938 at Jabal Dhahran. The Arabian American Oil Company, or Aramco (founded by some U.S. oil companies), soon began drilling wells, constructing pipelines, and creating harbors for oil tankers. King Ibn Saud, as Abdulaziz had become known, gave them permission to do this in exchange for royalties, or

King Ibn Saud met with many world leaders in the 1940s, including President Franklin Roosevelt of the United States.

payments, on the oil they were pumping. These payments seemed huge to the once-poor country and formed the basis of Saudi Arabia's new-found wealth.

The world no longer ignored the Desert Kingdom. Important leaders from around the world began to meet with King Ibn Saud. They wanted to discuss the problems of the Middle East with the head of oil-rich Saudi Arabia.

When King Ibn Saud died in 1953, his oldest son, Saud, became king. This followed the pattern of royal succession in countries such as England: When the ruler of the country dies, that person's oldest son or daughter becomes the ruler. (However, when Saud stepped down as king, in 1964, the Al Saud family decided to make as king, not

Saud's oldest son, but Ibn Saud's next son in line, Faisal. Thus King Ibn Saud's sons would each be king in turn.)

It had been the practice of this royal family to train its sons from an early age to become leaders. For example, after World War I, King Ibn Saud sent his fourteen-year-old son Faisal to represent Saudi Arabia at meetings in London. It may be hard to imagine a fourteen-year-old representing his nation at important meetings, but he did just fine. When he met King George V of England, Prince Faisal exchanged swords with the British ruler and showed a dignity that he would have throughout his life. The family made sure that all the sons gained leadership experience. The princes ruled the country's cities, provinces, army, navy, air force, and large businesses.

The Rule of King Faisal

In 1964, eleven years after King Saud had become Saudi Arabia's leader, it was clear how the royal family operated. In that year the family decided that Saud should step down in favor of his younger brother Faisal. The family felt that Faisal was better suited to help Saudi Arabia solve some financial problems that had arisen. Saud did step down, and Saudi Arabia had a new ruler, King Faisal.

King Faisal immediately showed himself to be an outstanding leader. Under King Saud, Saudi Arabia's money situation had grown steadily worse. King Faisal set up strict budgets, and in a year and a half, the country was out of trouble. Besides improving other things for his own country he also helped other countries in the Middle East form strong governments. He used his influence against Egypt, which had formed a socialist government and was trying to help people in the Middle East set up other socialist governments. King Faisal felt this type of government was against the laws of Islam, and he fought the trend.

Because oil was priced low by Aramco and other foreign drilling companies, more and more countries began importing oil from the Desert Kingdom in ever-increasing amounts. At the same time, Saudi Arabia and other oil-rich countries began demanding more of a voice in the production and pricing of their oil. By 1973, King Faisal had a much greater say in running Aramco. He would find a way to use this new influence as a weapon in that year.

The Arabs of the Middle East were opposed to the setting up of the State of Israel after World War II. A Jewish state in Palestine had been promised to European Jews by Britain and some other nations. The Arabs believed that setting up such a state in Palestine would uproot thousands of Arab Palestinians who had lived there for many, many years. Arab leaders regretted the fact that millions of Jews had been killed in Nazi concentration camps during World War II, but they did not feel they had done anything to cause that slaughter. Also, Jerusalem is another city holy to Muslims, and they did not want it under Israeli control.

Israel was founded despite Arab protests, and trouble immediately followed. The Arabs and Israelis fought three wars: in 1948 (just after the State of Israel was set up), in 1967, and in 1973. These wars have added a great deal of formerly Arab land to Israel, increasing the hard feelings between Arabs and Israelis.

Over the years, Saudi Arabia supplied the Arab side, the Palestinians, with every kind of assistance, especially money. But when the 1973 Arab-Israeli war broke out, King Faisal of Saudi Arabia decided to use Saudi influence in another way. He cut off the supply of Saudi oil to the United States and other nations that supported Israel.

As a result of that cut-off of oil, long lines of cars with empty fuel tanks formed at gas stations in the United States, England, France, the Netherlands, and many other countries throughout the world. People had to think twice about driving large "gas-guzzling" automobiles, since they used so much fuel. The price of gasoline shot up; in the United States gas went from 50 cents a gallon to more than $1 a gallon. King Faisal eventually resumed the flow of oil from his country to the United States, but Americans now knew how dependent they had become on Saudi Arabia.

Then, in 1975, with no warning, a young Saudi man shot and killed King Faisal for reasons that are still not

Oil gave Saudi Arabia a great deal of bargaining power in the world. Here, natural gas is burned off near an oil-drilling site.

clear. Some think that it was an act of revenge. (The young man's brother had been killed by soldiers as he was protesting the opening of a television station in Riyadh.) Whatever the reason, the nation and the world mourned the loss of a great Arab leader, a deeply religious man who felt very close to his people.

Some nations have a hard time transferring power peacefully to a new leader. But Saudi Arabia remained calm. Its people watched as Prince Khalid, second in charge, took over the government, and they gave him their loyalty. The same was true when King Fahd took over in 1982, upon Khalid's death.

Saudi–United States Relations

Over the years, Saudi Arabia and other OPEC countries had demanded a greater voice in how their oil businesses were run. They did not want all the oil to be taken and their countries to be poor again. Soon, some of the countries nationalized, or took total control of their oil industries. Aramco was nationalized in 1980; Saudis now managed every part of their oil business.

The United States and Saudi Arabia have remained close, despite their disagreements about Israel. The Americans and Saudis are both against Communism and together would oppose any attempts by Russia or any other country to take over Middle Eastern oil fields. In a sense, both countries have come to depend on each other. While the United States—and a good part of the Western world—needs Saudi oil to run factories, cars, and airplanes, Saudi Arabia needs United States technology and skill in building cities in order to get ready for the twenty-first century.

An example of Saudi–United States cooperation occurred in 1990, when Iraqi troops invaded Kuwait and threatened to take over the oil fields of Saudi Arabia to the south. When the Saudi leader, King Fahd, asked the United States for help, President George Bush and other leaders, including those from Arab countries such as Egypt and Syria, sent troops to the area. During the subsequent Persian Gulf War, which began in January 1991, those troops joined Saudi troops to drive out the Iraqis from Kuwait and free that country. The commander of the western troops, General Norman Schwarzkopf, knew the Middle East well, having lived in Iran and traveled to Saudi Arabia as a boy, when his father was stationed in the Middle East.

Planning the Future

The vast supply of oil under Saudi Arabia's sands will run out eventually, probably within the next hundred years. To prepare themselves for that day, the Saudis have begun to look for other sources of income. They have reopened a gold mine and begun looking for other minerals in the mountains and desert. They have started a program to grow enough wheat for their own needs. They have built large factories to make such products as concrete and fertilizer to sell to the rest of the world. And they continue to invest vast sums of money in other parts of the world.

In these ways, the Saudis hope to be ready for the day when the oil stops flowing out of the desert. By that time the country will have become one of the richest in the history of the world. That's quite a change from the days when it was one of the poorest.

The most amazing part of this development is the speed with which it is taking place. For centuries, Arabia minded its own business, raised sheep and camels, and helped the pilgrims on their way to the holy cities of Mecca and Medina. The rest of the world just ignored it. In the last fifty years, though, Saudi Arabia has become one of the most important nations in the world because of its oil. The country is now rushing to enter the twenty-first century. In doing so, it wants to learn from other countries, imitating what is good and avoiding what is bad. It will continue to be a deeply religious nation, with hopes of sharing its good qualities with other nations.

THE SPOKEN STORY

Saudis love their nation, their religion, their families and relatives—and their language. One of their proverbs indicates how strongly they feel about language, especially spoken language: "The sword wounds the body, but words wound the soul." To the Saudis, words pack a powerful punch and can help or harm, depending on how people use them.

For hundreds of years in the Arabian Peninsula, the Arabs depended on the spoken word. This was long before radio and television and even before the use of books. The Arabs used the spoken word to converse, to pass on knowledge from generation to generation, and to worship God.

Today, some 200 million people in various parts of the world speak Arabic. Many of these people use Arabic because they are Muslims. They believe that God himself used Arabic to speak to their prophet Muhammad. The holy book of Islam, the Qur'an, is written in the Arabic language.

Arabic differs from English in several important ways. For example, while English and other languages, such as German and French, are written from left to right, Arabic is written from right to left. And Arabic has a flowing, rounded alphabet in which each letter of a word is connected to the next letter of that word.

The Arabic language bases each of its words on a three-consonant combination. All the words related to one idea will have the same three consonants. For example, all the Arabic words that deal with writing have the consonants k-t-b, in that order. Thus the Arabic words for "book," "typist," "library," and "write" all contain k-t-b. Arabic varies the words by adding one or more of its three short vowels and three long vowels. A nice thing about this system is that, once you learn the basic three consonants for any idea, you can easily learn all the words related to that idea.

Arabic Loanwords in English

When people who speak two different languages come in contact, each group will often borrow words and phrases from the other's language. The English language has given a number of words to Arabic. English, in turn,

This beautifully written phrase says "The Kingdom of Saudi Arabia" in Arabic Script.

has taken many words from Arabic, for example, *baseball, soda,* and *television.* This has happened over many centuries.

For example, the word for "the" in Arabic is *al.* Several Arabic words that have come into English have come with the word *al*; examples are *alcohol, alcove,* and *algebra.* The letters *a-l* at the end of our word *admiral* also come from the word *the* in Arabic and, in fact, must have come from a phrase that meant something like "commander of the sea." However, the word for "sea" was lost along the way, so our word *admiral* means "commander of the." A few other common English words from Arabic are *cotton, giraffe, lime, mummy, sherbet, sofa,* and *sugar.* As Arabs and Americans continue to get to know one another, their languages will blend in new ways, too.

We also borrowed our number system from the Arabs, who got it many centuries ago from the Hindus of India. The Arabs later went on to use a different system, but many countries of the world still use what we call Arabic numerals.

*The top line shows the numbers used by the Saudis today;
below them are our present-day Arabic numerals.*

*Parts of the Qur'an are often copied in lovely calligraphy
and displayed as decorations.*

Ways to Communicate

The Islamic religion discourages the use of pictures
that show animals or the human figure whether in
photographs or drawings. Islam does this in order to
prevent the worship of humans, a form of idolatry.

Muslim artists over the years have therefore not used
human or animal figures in their paintings. Instead they
used geometric patterns. They also made designs using the
letters of the Arabic language. The beautiful, elegant hand-
writing that they developed is called calligraphy.
Calligraphy was used to write holy books and also to
decorate mosques and other buildings.

Besides speaking and writing words, Saudis use hand
gestures to get across their meanings. In a way, they speak

not only with their mouths, but also with their eyes and their hands. Probably the most common gesture is putting the tips of the fingers and thumb together, pointing them upward, and moving the hand up and down. This means "Be patient" or "Wait a minute." The driver of a car will sometimes use this to the driver behind who insists on horn-tooting to get the traffic moving.

To get someone to come to them, people put their fingers together, point them downward, and shake their hands toward themselves. When people pull their chins, it means they are not happy with something a child has done. It means "Shame on you!"

If a mechanic or someone with dirty hands meets you, the person will extend the right wrist to you in place of the dirty hand. The wrist is taken and shaken in the normal way.

There are some things that no one should do in Saudi Arabia. One is never to offer something to someone with the left hand. As in many places outside the United States, the Saudis do not use their left hands when eating or shaking hands. Another impolite act is to show the sole of one's shoe to an Arab—for example, when sitting down. That is a sign of disrespect.

When two Arab men meet after an absence of some weeks, they will often kiss each other on the cheek. When Saudis meet their king, they will sometimes kiss him on the nose or on the shoulder as a mark of great respect. You might be surprised to see men or boys holding hands as they walk on the street. This only means that they are good friends. Arabs like to touch people more than Americans do. They like to get close to their friends, even to smell them, since they believe that each person has a distinctive smell.

For Fun

The Saudis like to play with words and sounds. They especially like riddles or word puzzles. In a favorite riddle, a person is asked what this describes: If we take from it, it will become bigger; if we put something in it, it will become smaller. Can you guess what it is? A hole.

The stories that the Saudis like best, though, deal with such qualities as bravery, generosity, and unselfishness. For example, they tell the story of a great Bedouin chief by the name of Hatim Tai.

Everyone who met Hatim Tai remarked on how generous he was with whatever he had. People who had never met Hatim could hardly believe all the stories they heard. Once a wealthy man in another country heard about Hatim from some friends.

"I don't believe Hatim is as generous as people say he is. Tell me what his most valuable possession is," said the man.

Arabs are used to touching their friends; even men friends sometimes hold hands as they walk along.

"His horse has to be his most valuable possession," the man's friends said. "Even Hatim's enemies have not tried to get his horse because they respect his great affection for the animal."

"Just how valuable is this horse?" the man asked.

"It is the swiftest horse in all of Arabia," they answered. "Hatim raised the horse with his family, has never spoken a harsh word to it, has never even used a whip or spur when riding it. It would be a great insult to even ask Hatim what price he would sell the horse for."

After thinking for a short time, the man responded: "I will not ask what the selling price of the horse is. Instead, I will ask Hatim to give the horse to me as a gift. If he refuses, as I know he will, we will tell the world how selfish this Hatim really is. I will send my servants to Hatim's camp to ask this favor."

And so the man's servants traveled to Hatim's camp to do their master's bidding. It was a long, difficult journey to the distant place. After twenty hard days of rain and little food, the servants finally reached the place where Hatim and a few of his followers had recently pitched their tents.

When Hatim saw how wet, hungry, and tired the travelers were, he immediately gave them warm, dry clothing from his own supply and arranged for them to sleep in the best part of his large tent. After some delay, Hatim had them sit down to a huge feast of delicious meat,

*The desert and the heroes who lived in it figure
in many Saudi legends.*

all carefully roasted and made into delicious soups and dishes. That night the visitors slept very soundly.

In the morning the visitors confessed to Hatim why they had come. "O generous Hatim," they said, "our master has sent us here on a terrible mission. Everyone who has known you has boasted of your goodness and generosity. Our master did not believe that any man could be so good and so has sent us to ask for your magnificent horse as a gift for him."

Hatim could not believe his ears. He shook his head in amazement and answered: "My friends, if only you had told me of this mission when you first arrived last night. You could not have known that I was not prepared for guests last night, that the rest of my followers—with goats and sheep and oxen—would arrive in a day or two.

"When you came to my tent last evening," he continued, "I could see that you were cold and wet and hungry. And yet I had no goats or sheep or oxen to offer you at dinner. I could not have you go away from here still hungry. Go back now to your cruel master and tell him that last night I cooked my beautiful, strong horse for your supper."

FESTIVALS AND FOODS

Saudi Arabia does not have as many holidays or festivals as other countries, but it takes great pride in the ones it does celebrate. The Saudis don't seem to miss the great number of holidays that other countries have. They visit with each other quite a bit and do a lot of things with their families throughout the year.

One holiday that Saudis enjoy celebrating is called *Id al-Adha*, the Feast of the Sacrifice, in which families will sacrifice a lamb or a goat and then share the meat with neighbors and the poor. The holiday is celebrated during the pilgrimage time, when many Muslims from around the world visit the holy cities of Mecca and Medina.

Children look forward to the Feast of the Sacrifice because of the delicious food and good times they have while visiting their friends. In the morning, they join their mothers and older brothers' wives to visit some women friends in the village and wish them a "Happy Festival." While the women talk among themselves and drink some hot coffee or tea, the children get to eat some tasty small cakes. Meanwhile, fathers visit some of the other men to exchange best wishes and to find out the latest news. Many people in the town put out the colorful green-and-white Saudi flag in honor of the special day.

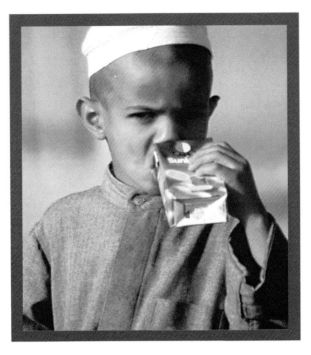

A young boy pauses for a drink of juice while playing in the park.

The children usually get to spend some time in a local park, where they can use the swings and slides. On one side of the park, the women continue their visiting. On the other side, the men talk among themselves and drink coffee.

Most families try to cook a whole sheep on this special holiday. They then share this with those people who cannot afford a sheep that year. The women cook rice and vegetables to go along with the meat. They also provide the large flat pieces of Arab, or pita, bread that everyone likes to dip into the meat sauce.

Id al-Adha may last several days. A village will have a lot to celebrate if several of its members have made the pilgrimage to the holy cities of Mecca and Medina.

When a friend or relative makes a pilgrimage to Mecca as these Muslims have, there is special rejoicing in that person's town and family.

The Fasting Month

A second religious holiday, *Id al-Fitr*, the Feast of the Breaking of the Fast, follows *Ramadan*, the month of fasting. During Ramadan, all Muslims—except the young, the sick, and those on long journeys—have to fast. From sunrise to sundown, they do not eat or drink anything at all. Most people continue to work or go to school during those days, but they work a little less vigorously than normal because they can have nothing to eat or drink until sundown. Since the Islamic calendar has shorter months than our calendar, the month of Ramadan occurs at different times of the year. Sometimes it falls during the long, hot days of summer—and that can cause a lot of hardship for everyone.

The fasting is to remind the Muslims about God and the spiritual life. It helps them toughen their bodies for hard times, something they've had a lot of in the past. They also begin to understand the suffering that poor people go through every day of their lives. The Saudis remember that their country was once counted among the poor nations of the world.

At sundown the sound of a cannon or drum call to prayer signals the end of that day's fasting. The whole family gathers for a most welcome meal. First, they have some dates, water, and Arab coffee. Next, they eat soup, fried meat pies, mashed beans, bread, and salad. Then they have dessert, different kinds of fruit, juices, hot tea, and more Arab coffee. Such a meal seems to taste better after a long day without food or drink. It is a happy occasion, full of good cheer and friendliness. A cannon is fired or a drum is beaten just before dawn, too. Then everyone has a chance to eat one last morsel of food before the fasting begins again.

In some towns, the usual activities of night and day are reversed. People sometimes rest during the daylight hours especially if Ramadan comes in summer. Then at night, after sharing their hearty meals with their families, they might go out to do their shopping or visiting until late at night.

It is with real joy that Id al-Fitr is welcomed at the end of Ramadan. The Feast of the Breaking of the Fast may last several days. Sometimes during these feasts all the families of a town will get together and share their food with everyone else there. A special dish that families prepare is roasted whole lamb stuffed with rice or macaroni, dried dates and apricots, and different types of nuts. Families spend these special days together and visit friends to wish them a blessed holiday.

Yet another special day is National Day, September 23. This holiday celebrates the uniting of the country under the name of Saudi Arabia. Schools and stores usually stay open on this day, since it is not as important as the two religious holidays.

The King's Holidays

Sometimes a town will have a special holiday when the Saudi king pays a visit. The people look up to the royal family, and so they celebrate on the day the king visits their town. He tries to visit as many Saudi towns and cities as possible each year in order to keep in close touch with his people. When he does visit, the people will decorate the town with thousands of lights and welcome signs. These visits give everyone in the towns a chance to see their king and talk with him instead of having to go to the capital city of Riyadh to meet him.

Sometimes an important person from another country comes to Saudi Arabia for an official visit. It might be a king, or a queen, or a president. Then local officials will put up the flag of the visitor's country all through the town. Sometimes the guests are driven around in limousines to call on different officials.

Because Saudi Arabia is such a dry country, with no rain at all in some years in parts of the country, the king from time to time will set aside a few days as prayer days. He asks all the people to spend those days praying for rain to fall on the dry land. On such prayer days, especially after many months of no rain, schools and shops may close, at least for part of the day, while the Saudis go to the mosques to pray.

On a number of occasions throughout the year, especially when a large group of men gathers, you can see a very unusual dance—the *Ardah*, or sword dance. It begins when several men with small drums and tambourines start playing their instruments, often around a large Saudi flag flying from a pole fixed in the ground. Then a group of men, carrying either long swords or rifles, gathers around the flag. Sometimes singers join the group, link arms, and face each other in two long lines. The singers start chanting different verses as they sway back and forth.

Then the men carrying swords or rifles begin a slow walk around the flagpole, in step with the beating of the drums. They swing their swords or rifles over their heads in slow motion. The more experienced men throw their swords or rifles high into the air, catching them as they fall. The excitement grows as the sword dance goes on and on. If the king or princes are present, they will join in the dancing. The sing-song chant and the slow-motion dance make the Ardah a most unusual sight.

Favorite Feasts

After such vigorous exercise as the Ardah, the men gather for a meal. Whenever guests are present, the girls and women of a family stay in another room, preparing food and keeping out of sight. If the boys of the family join the men for the meal, they remain silent unless spoken to, to show respect for their elders.

The meal, a typical mid-afternoon Saudi meal, usually consists of rice and meat. In the middle of the room, on a large tablecloth spread over rugs on the floor, a large bowl of steaming white rice will be placed. Chunks of roasted lamb or camel meat, mixed with onions and nuts, then top the rice. All around the bowl of rice and meat are bowls of vegetables—perhaps roasted eggplant or potatoes.

As the men eat, they sit on the floor with their legs crossed. They all take rice from the same large bowl, using only their right hands to pick up small portions of rice mixed with the delicious stew. They roll the rice up into small balls and pop the balls into their mouths. Often there will be a bowl of yogurt with a spoon at the side of each person's plate.

Toward the end of the meal, the host brings out fresh apples or oranges and maybe some dates. Later the men usually drink the rich, strong coffee they like so much. They drink it without milk or sugar and from small cups that have no handles. When a guest has had enough coffee, he will shake the cup from side to side to indicate that he's done.

The Saudis enjoy feasting very much, and over the years they have developed favorite foods for each of the

Coffee and tea are prepared by the host and offered to guests at the end of a meal.

main meals. For breakfast they often have bread, cheese, yogurt, milk, olives, eggs, some mashed beans, hot tea, and Arab coffee. They like to have breakfast at about 7:00 A.M., just before the children head off to school and the father goes off to his workplace.

The family has lunch, the main Saudi meal of the day, around 2:00 or 3:00 P.M., right after the children come home from school and the father returns from his work. Then the family members sit down for a big meal of rice, salad, meat—lamb, chicken, or beef—some vegetables, pita bread, fruit, hot tea or coffee, and maybe even some

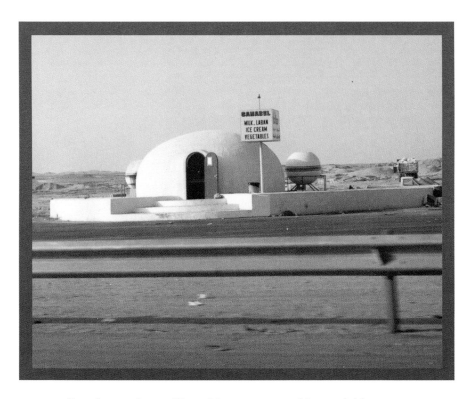

*People can buy milk and ice cream at this roadside store,
which is shaped like an igloo.*

cold soft drinks. (Pork and alcoholic drinks are both
forbidden by the Qur'an.) This is a special time of the day,
when members of the family tell the others about the
morning's events and get ready for an afternoon nap, some
homework, a little television watching, or a return to work.

Later in the evening, around 9:00 or even 10:00 P.M.,
the family will have a light dinner. They might have bread,
cheese, olives, and perhaps some soup. Families in many
parts of the world prefer such a light meal at this time
because they will be going to bed in a few hours.

Tabbouleh is a popular Middle Eastern salad. Perhaps you'd like to try making it.

Tabbouleh

1 cup bulgur wheat (found in some supermarkets and in health food stores)

1/3 cup chopped fresh parsley (or 1/4 cup dried)

1/4 cup finely chopped fresh mint leaves (or 3 tablespoons dried)

1/3 cup onion, finely chopped

1 small clove of garlic, crushed

1 medium tomato, cut into chunks

1 medium cucumber, scrubbed and cut into chunks

1 tablespoon olive oil

Juice of 1 medium-size lemon

Salt

1. Put the bulgur wheat in a large bowl. Cover the grain with water so that there is 1/2 inch of water over the grain. Let the bulgur soak up all the water. It will be soft and chewy when the water has been absorbed, in an hour to an hour and a half.

2. Combine the parsley and mint with the bulgur, mixing them thoroughly. Add the onion and garlic and mix again. Then mix in the tomato and cucumber.

3. Drizzle the olive oil and lemon juice over the whole salad, and mix everything very thoroughly. Add salt to taste, if you wish, and mix again.

4. Cover your tabbouleh and allow it to stand for an hour or so in the refrigerator to let the flavor develop. Serves 6.

Tabbouleh can be served on a lettuce leaf—a holder that can be eaten with the salad. Or you can use Arab bread, or pita. This handy pocket bread can be cut in half and filled with lettuce and tabbouleh for a salad sandwich!

FAMILY

Next to the Islamic religion, the most important part of Saudi society is the family. The word *family* means more than just a father, mother, and children under one roof. It also includes uncles, aunts, and cousins who live nearby. Often in Saudi Arabian towns, relatives will live near each other for protection from rival tribes and companionship, and out of a genuine love for each other. In many cases a Saudi will grow up, attend school, get married, settle down, and die in the same town. Like many people from Asia and Africa, the Saudis tend to stay in one place all their lives. As they say: "Trees often transplanted seldom prosper."

Lately, more and more people have been moving to the larger cities to seek education and work. Whole families may move around a bit more, but they still keep the close family ties that have existed for so long in Saudi Arabia. When Saudis say they will be visiting relatives, they often mean they will be going to the house next door.

Saudi Names

The Saudi father clearly rules his family. To see how important he is, we only need to look at his children's names. If the father's name is Abdullah, his son, Ahmad,

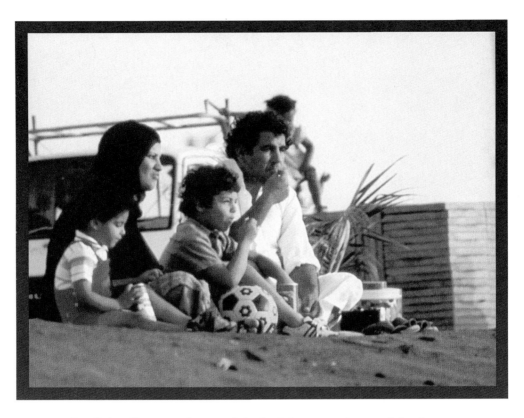

Saudi families spend a good deal of time together, and for fun they enjoy picnicking and playing in the desert.

will be called Ahmad bin Abdullah, which means "Ahmad, son of Abdullah." The complete name of a man will give you a short history of his family.

Thus, King Fahd's official name is as follows: Fahd bin Abdulaziz bin Abdurrahman bin Faisal bin Turki bin Abdullah bin Muhammad bin Saud. The Arabic word *bin* means "son of," and so King Fahd's name means "Fahd, (who is the) son of Abdulaziz, (who is the) son of Abdurrahman," and so on.

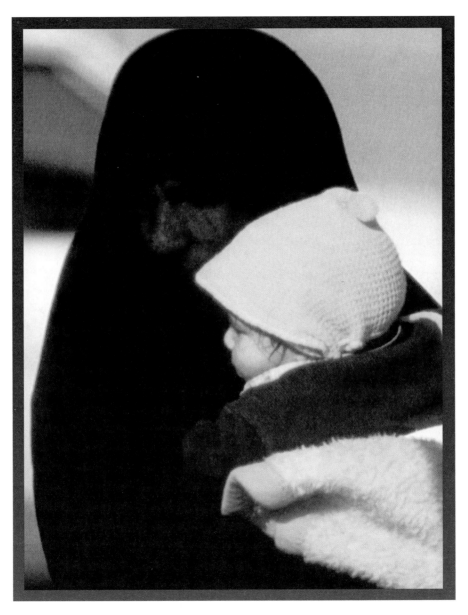

Children are very important to Saudi parents. Here a woman in a black aba and a veil bundles up her baby to protect him from the strong desert wind.

On the other hand, the birth of a child, especially a son, means so much to a family that the parents may become known by the child's name. For example, if a man named Hisham has a son by the name of Saad, the man could become known as Abu Saad, or "Father of Saad." Saad's mother would be known as Umm Saad, "Mother of Saad." If their first child is a girl, they may use the girl's name until their first son is born.

Women and Marriage

Women in Saudi Arabia clearly lead a more restricted life than men. They usually wear black veils and long black abas, or cloaks, when outside their homes and seldom attend social gatherings where men and women would be together. They do not attend classes with men or drive cars. If the police were ever to catch a woman driving, they would arrest her husband for allowing her to drive.

Very few women work at jobs outside the home. They usually stay at home, taking care of their families. In large, wealthy families they may have the help of one or more servants and cooks. Saudi women enjoy visiting with other women or, in the evening, going with their husbands or brothers to shop for different items like household goods, clothing, or jewelry.

The few Saudi women who do work outside the home either teach in girls' schools or work in maternity clinics or other places that serve only women. More and more girls are attending schools and universities in Saudi Arabia with hopes of becoming doctors, scientists, or social workers. Even if all of them don't reach these goals, the Saudi women of the future will have much more education than in the past.

Marriage is one of the most important parts of a Saudi's life. Islam allows a Muslim man to be married to four women at the same time, but he must treat them all equally. The practice of having more than one wife is dying out, however, partly because it can be very expensive to have several wives! Women can have only one husband at a time.

Men and women differ in several other ways when it comes to marriage. For example, it is much easier for a man to divorce his wife than for a woman to divorce her husband. Also, the Islamic religion allows Muslim men to marry women of other religions, but does not allow Muslim women to marry men of other religions. If a Muslim man does marry a woman of another religion, the woman does not have to change her religion. However, the couple must bring up their children as Muslims.

When Saudi women are in the privacy of their homes or in schools, they can take off their long abas and black veils and relax. At wedding parties, women will remain in one room, and the men will stay in an entirely different room. By themselves, the women get a chance to show their friends their newest outfits. Without men around, they are freer to be themselves and unwind.

At such wedding parties, however, unmarried women have to be on their toes. They try to be as pretty and witty as possible, since the sisters and mothers of single young men will be seeking the best possible women for wives for their brothers or sons.

Unmarried children usually live with their parents or relatives until marriage. When a young man feels ready for marriage, his parents will begin making preparations. The parents still usually arrange marriages in Saudi Arabia, which means trying to pick out the best persons for their marriageable children. However, if a son or daughter does not approve of the marriage choice, the parents will usually not force their child to marry that person. Until recently, most young women in Saudi Arabia got married between the ages of fourteen and sixteen. This is changing, however, as more and more young women attend universities and postpone marriage for a few years.

When two people do marry, the groom pays a sum of money to his bride's family. This could be several thousand dollars or more, depending on his own finances and the importance of the bride's family. In the past, when people did not have a lot of cash, a man often paid for his bride with a certain number of camels or sheep.

Cousins sometimes marry each other, if everyone agrees. This took place in the past more frequently than it does now. Then, if a young man had to give his bride's family some camels or sheep, it would be better, people felt, if he married a cousin from the same tribe and kept the camels in his tribe. If he married a girl from another tribe, he would have to give his animals, which were more valuable than money, to the other tribe.

Clothes for Desert and City

Approaching marriage, a young man relies on his family to pick out the best wife for him. He himself can't tell what the women look like, since they all look alike in their black veils and abas.

Muslim men also dress modestly and simply. In Western countries, men may compete with each other to see who can buy the fanciest suit or the nicest pair of shoes, but not so in Saudi Arabia. Saudi men wear long, simple outer garments called thawbs, which go from their necks to their ankles. In winter the thawb is made of gray or black wool to keep out the cold desert wind; in summer it is made of white cotton to reflect the sun's rays.

When these girls are older, they probably will also wear veils and the long black abas over their clothes, as do their mothers.

On his head a Saudi man wears a large piece of material called the kaffiyeh, which he can wrap around his face in case of a sandstorm. It is usually a red-and-white checkered wool material in the winter and a white cotton material in the summer. A thick black ropelike band holds the kaffiyeh in place. (In the past, this band was put around two of a camel's feet to keep the camel from straying. Even though this is not done any more, the tradition of wearing this band continues.) The kaffiyeh can protect a man's head from both cold wind and the hot sun.

Muslim men do not wear gold ornaments or silk outfits. The simplicity of the large thawb allows men to do their bowing and kneeling easily during their daily prayers. Western-style clothing might be less comfortable because of its closer fit. Boys tend to dress like their fathers, and older girls dress like their mothers. With such simple styles, everyday clothing takes up just a small part of a family's budget.

Life in the Cities

In the big cities of Saudi Arabia, such as Riyadh, the capital, and Jidda on the Red Sea, activities are much the same as in any big city. Buses crowd the streets, taxis toot their horns, and cars make their way along busy roads. On their way home from school, boys may stop for a quick game of soccer or a bike ride along the busy streets. They often have chores to complete at home, as do the girls. And, of course, there's always homework from school to keep them busy.

A family often has its big meal of the day when the children come home from school and the father comes home from work. After eating, each family member will probably take a long nap. The father usually returns to work at his business or shop in the late afternoon for several hours. The afternoon nap breaks up the day and seems to make it last longer into the evening.

The cities and towns have no movie theaters, so families often spend the evenings visiting with their friends, going to city parks, or watching television. On weeknights the children usually go to bed early so as to be ready for a new day. The weekend days in Saudi Arabia are Thursday and Friday. That's because Friday is the Saudis' special day of worship, as Sunday is in many Western countries. Saturday, then, starts a new week, and Wednesday ends the school week.

For fun, Saudi people like to go shopping. They can choose a large shopping center or an old-time market, called a *suq*. In these suqs you can usually find shops that sell just one type of item, such as cloth, paint, books, or gold. Sometimes you'll find a section of town where all the shops sell used furniture. Another section of town will have many toy stores or clothing stores.

In these old-fashioned marketplaces, many objects may not have prices on them. Instead, the customer has to ask, "How much is this shirt?" or "How much is that neck-lace?" When the storekeeper states his price, bargaining—the fun part of shopping—begins.

Customer: "How much is that pen?"

Shopkeeper: "Ten riyals."

Customer: "That's too expensive. The shop down the street sells the same pen for just five riyals."

Shopkeeper: "I don't believe you, but because you

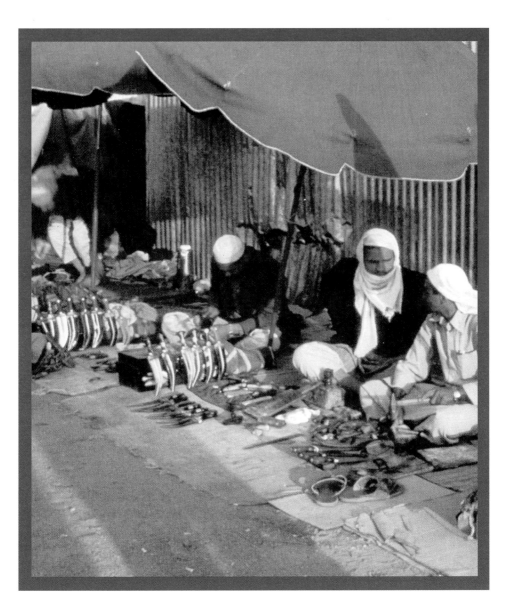

*Bargaining goes on today in old-fashioned markets and anywhere
a small shop is set up.*

seem like a nice person and I'm in a very generous mood today, you can have the pen for eight riyals."

Customer: "You must be kidding! It probably doesn't write very well and will stain my shirt pocket. I'll give you six riyals for it."

Shopkeeper: "I guarantee that it is the best pen for the money. All right. Give me a mere seven riyals and it's yours."

And so the customer gets the pen for a good price. Bargaining challenges the customer to match wits with shopkeepers and also takes a good bit of time. Most Saudis seem to enjoy bargaining for almost everything. It becomes a kind of game between the shopkeeper and his customer. The merchant will often look his customer up and down very carefully before deciding what he thinks the customer will pay for the item.

In the big supermarkets, the prices are clearly marked and so there is no bargaining, but it still goes on in the old-time markets. As old ways die out, the fine art of bargaining will probably pass out of fashion, but—while it lasts—it can be fun.

night. This is called the oral tradition—the passing on of knowledge by word of mouth.

The few schools in the big towns were run by the mosque, the religious center of the town. The boys who went to these schools learned some arithmetic and a lot of religion. They also learned penmanship, or the art of carefully making their Arabic letters. The letters would lead to studying Arabic grammar and then to reading the Qur'an.

Unlike other Middle Eastern countries, Saudi Arabia had no missionary schools, or schools set up and run by Christian priests and ministers. Countries such as Egypt and Lebanon allowed missionary schools to open in many towns and cities, and these became very important in teaching thousands of their people. Saudi Arabia, however, did not want any non-Muslim schools in the country.

Schools in a Hurry

Recently, the Saudi government decided to educate all of its citizens. It began building schools in a hurry; in the 1980s, a new school was opened every week in the rush to give every Saudi the chance at a good education. Sometimes the government used buildings that once had other purposes; for example, it made schools out of old railway stations. In big cities, it built large air-conditioned schools with the most modern equipment.

Unlike Saudi children of the past, these youngsters have the opportunity to go to school.

The country needed teachers at all levels, so Saudi Arabia brought in thousands of teachers from other countries, especially Egypt. Several universities were opened so that graduates from the high schools could become teachers, scientists, and doctors. For those students who wanted to become mechanics or farmers or auto mechanics, the government set up special vocational schools. These schools are especially important, since the many oil fields in the country require Saudis to work on both the oil rigs and the large oil tankers that take the oil to other countries.

When youngsters reach the age of six, they begin attending six years of elementary school, where they study the Islamic religion, arithmetic, Arabic, geography, history, and science. The girls also study cooking and sewing, and the boys have physical education. Boys and girls attend separate schools, beginning with elementary school at age six.

More and more parents want their children to go to school. They realize that the more education a person has, the better job that person can obtain. And so almost nine out of ten boys of first-grade age attend school. Many more girls attend school now than in the past, but not in as great numbers as the boys.

After elementary school, students have three years at intermediate school, in which they study the same subjects they studied in elementary school, as well as the English

Language studies are stressed in Saudi schools. The young student here is looking at a class project—an Arabic-language newspaper.

language. After that they're ready for high school. There they continue to study Islam and Arabic as well as science, mathematics, and English.

If you could visit a Saudi high school, especially when some classes are studying English, you would hear students working on English phrases and words. The students usually learn English in modern language laboratories, in which they use headphones to listen to tapes of English speakers. Saudi students have great memories and listening skills, and they can remember long passages or lists of words. This goes back to the time when there were not many books around, and people had to memorize parts of the Qur'an.

Boys and girls do not attend school together. Even at a university, the young men go to one part of the city for their classes, and the young women go to another part. Men teach the males, and women teach the females. If there is no woman teacher available for women students, a man can teach them by closed-circuit television. The students can see and talk to him, but he cannot see them.

All Sorts of Students

The Saudi government pays particular attention to those children who are blind, deaf, or handicapped in some way. These children go to special schools where they learn skills that will help them get good jobs. Teachers with special training teach these students skills such as rug weaving and furniture building as well as the basic subjects of reading and writing, including Braille for blind students. The items these students make are of such high quality that they sell for good prices in stores.

The government also has a rule that any company with more than fifty workers has to hire a certain number of disabled employees. Some countries try to hide their blind, deaf, and mentally handicapped children, but Saudi Arabia does not. It does its best to educate them and train them to do well in life.

The Saudi government tries to provide education and jobs to all Saudis. Young people sometimes work in their parents' businesses, as this boy does in his father's pottery business.

Sometimes it seems that almost everyone goes to school in Saudi Arabia. Many adults attend class in the evening after they have finished working in their shops or offices. They learn religion, reading, writing, mathematics, and other subjects. The government wants every Saudi to be able to read and write by the year 2000. The Prophet Muhammad told his followers to "seek knowledge from the cradle to the grave." That is just what modern Saudis are doing.

If a student goes to a university, the government will pay the student the equivalent of several hundred dollars each month to keep studying. If a student wants to study in another country, the government will pay for that, too. Most of those students who go to other countries for further study return to Saudi Arabia to take their places in businesses or schools and help other Saudis. Hundreds of returning students, having gained the latest information in science, medicine, computers, or business, are now helping the country as a whole take its rightful place in the world.

When students finish studying at a high school or a university, the government will often try to get them jobs that fit them just right. If they want to set up their own businesses, the government will lend them money. If they want to work in schools or offices, it will try to find them the best places. The Saudis have this saying about school and work: "A learned man without work is like a cloud without rain."

Because the government and parents are encouraging the children to learn all they can in school and to get as much education as possible, Saudi youngsters have come a long way in just a few short years. The grandchildren of sheep herders and camel drivers have become doctors, scientists, teachers, and business owners. It is no wonder that Saudi Arabia takes such great pride in what so many of its people have accomplished.

RACING ON CAMELS, HUNTING WITH BIRDS

Picture the following: Over 2,500 camels are racing across the desert, each camel ridden by a young Arab boy determined to win fame and a small fortune. Great clouds of dust rise from the thousands of camel hooves. People on the sidelines cheer for their favorite riders. The distance seems quite long, about 12 miles (19 kilometers), and many camels don't finish the race. But rich prizes await those riders who do.

Such a race takes place each spring in the desert outside of the capital city of Riyadh. For weeks before the big day, the boys feed their camels a special mixture of barley, corn, grass, and alfalfa. Each day they exercise their camels and train them to run as fast as possible.

Camels, however, are not made in such a way as to keep riders on their backs. The camel's hump forces the jockey to ride toward its back, a very difficult task that ends in some boys falling off. Even after months of practice, camels and riders sometimes part during the race, disappointing the youngsters who had dreamed of doing well.

The king awards prizes to the first 200 camel riders to finish. The boy who comes in first wins a gold dagger,

The exciting yearly camel race outside Riyadh draws many spectators.

$15,000 in Saudi riyals, a water-tank truck for use in the desert, and the reputation of being the best camel rider—at least for that year. Such a prize can help a Bedouin family buy a small herd of animals or purchase many of the items its members have dreamed about. The yearly camel race attracts hundreds of spectators, including many princes from the royal family. It becomes a very dusty afternoon as the racing camels stir up the desert sand, but the excitement and festivities of the day make it memorable for everyone who attends.

Far different in feel are the weekly horse races held in the winter and early spring, before the heat of the summer makes racing too difficult. A carefully tended racetrack in Riyadh provides the setting for the jockeys, their horses, and many spectators. The government does not allow any betting at these horse races, but many people turn out to see the exciting races and to cheer on the horses. One member of the royal family usually awards a trophy to the winning jockey at the end of the races. Many Saudi princes own horses, and they compete with each other in this expensive sport to see whose stable turns out the most winners.

Hunting With Birds

Another pastime that both the royal family and the more numerous Bedouins enjoy goes back hundreds of

A young jockey tends his camel after the big race.

years. At one time, Arabs used falcons to provide them with food. Desert nomads depended on animals such as rabbits and birds for their meals. Because these small animals could hide so easily in the desert, Bedouin hunters relied on their falcons to find and capture them. Today, this method of hunting is a sport—the sport of falconry.

Sometimes when you enter a Saudi village, you can see the preparations for a falcon hunt taking place. Before heading off to the desert for the hunt, the owner of the falcon puts a hood over the bird's head to keep it under control. He and his children then ride out into the desert, with the falcon sitting on the man's wrist.

When the hunter comes to a place where game might be found, he takes the hood off the falcon and releases it to soar into the sky and look for traces of the animals. When the high-flying falcon sights its prey, it will streak down at great speed to capture the rabbit or bird in its talons. The hunting bird keeps the captured animal under control until its master comes up to take it. Saudi Arabia is one of the last places in the world today where people still hunt with falcons. Because the price for these birds is often quite high, young boys in small villages raise and train falcons. They later sell them to wealthy hunters.

Hunting has always been a popular Saudi pastime. However, in 1977, the Saudi king banned the use of guns in hunting. Many animals such as ostriches and cheetahs were disappearing forever because of the widespread use of powerful hunting rifles. Animal lovers around the world hope that this will help protect the thousands of birds that migrate north each year from Africa, up along the Red Sea on the west coast of Saudi Arabia.

Popular Sports

Sports that are growing in popularity in Saudi Arabia include volleyball, swimming, archery, jujitso, basketball, and tennis. Each year more and more boys and girls take up these sports because they are fun and because they can help build strong, healthy bodies.

But, as in most of the world outside the United States, soccer has become the number one sport in Saudi Arabia. In many towns and cities, the country has built soccer fields including large stadiums for its national teams. Little by little, more and more youngsters are taking up the game at an early age. Nighttime lighting of playing fields further encourages the playing of soccer.

This national love for soccer has paid off. In 1984, Saudi Arabia sent its first national soccer team to the Olympics, held in Los Angeles. There it competed against some of the best soccer teams in the world. The Saudi team later won the 1989 World 16-Under title and was the runner up in the 1992 Asian Cup.

Western sports, such as volleyball, are becoming more popular among Saudis.

Sports for Sea and Sand

The water on either side of Saudi Arabia attracts many people who like to go swimming, boating, fishing, and scuba diving. (Saudi men and women don't usually swim together, but that doesn't prevent women from wading in the warm waters along the coasts!) Speedboats and sailboats are becoming more popular, especially with younger people who live near the coasts. Parents and teachers there, as in

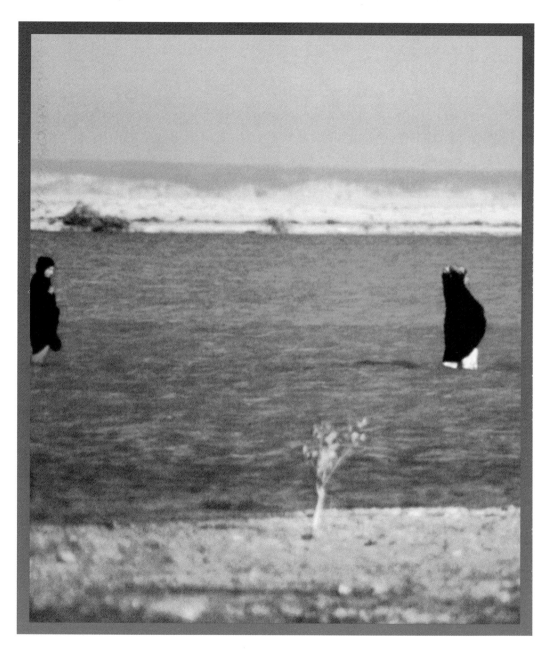

Even women in abas go wading for fun.

other countries, stress the safety rules of water sports,
since fast boats can be so dangerous. You can also find
more and more people taking up windsurfing, in which
they ride surfboards with sails attached to them. If you've
ever tried to ride a windsurfer, you know how difficult it
can be to keep standing up on one.

Fishing is attracting a growing number of sports
lovers. Along the coastline in Jidda on the Red Sea, piers
that jut out into the sea provide an easy way for fishermen
to get their lines out into the water. You can often see the
fish swimming among the pillars of these boardwalks,
ignoring the many baited lines hanging down!

Divers particularly like the Red Sea because the coral
reefs in it are home to some truly beautiful fish. If you
went snorkeling or scuba diving in the Red Sea, you might
see lovely butterfly fish, angel fish, or parrot fish.
However, you'd also have to look out for furry sea spiders,
dangerous eels, scorpion fish, and menacing sharks. You
might find some turtles swimming along, a porpoise or
two, and possibly even a whale.

Several of the more important sports in Saudi Arabia
have to do with the desert, as does much of life in that
country. Camel racing, horse racing, hunting with
falcons—all have their origins in the desert. And that is
fitting for a nation known to much of the world as the
Desert Kingdom.

*Many beautiful fish such as this lion-fish can be seen by divers
in the coral reefs of the Red Sea.*

Tents in the desert may be plain white or black or may be decorated with beautiful colors and patterns.

Some modern sports, such as racing dune buggies across sand dunes, also seem very suitable for that part of the world. You can also see runners jogging over the desert rather than in the big cities, since the cities are so crowded with cars and buses. Westerners introduced these sports to Saudi Arabia, and little by little the Saudis are taking them up.

One desert-related activity that many Saudi families do together is camping. On weekends you can see many tents out on the desert, each tent belonging to a family. The boys will often be playing soccer nearby, while the younger children may be gathering firewood.

If a family doesn't want to spend a whole weekend on the desert, they might choose at least to have a picnic there with their friends. They'll light a large bonfire to barbecue a sheep and light up the darkness while they tell the stories that children love to hear, and then they'll head back to the city when the picnic is over.

Before it gets too dark, they may take time out to look for dinosaur bones or "desert diamonds," which are quartz-type stones that sparkle like real diamonds. Some people have these stones cut and polished and made into pretty necklaces.

The peace and quiet of the sand dunes can help take people's minds off their problems. In a way, too, being in the desert causes many Saudis to think of earlier times, when their ancestors wandered over the desert, tending their flocks of animals. The past and the present can seem to merge on visits such as these.

THE ARAB WORLD IN THE UNITED STATES

When we look at the Saudis who have come to the United States, we must remember that, before 1932, there were no Saudis as such. In that year, King Ibn Saud established the modern nation of Saudi Arabia. Before that time, people of the Arabian Peninsula had a variety of names, because different empires controlled that land at different times. For example, the Ottoman Empire ruled the peninsula from the 1500s to about 1920. During that time, the people of the Arabian Peninsula were known as Ottomans or Turks. In later years, people there were called Yemenis or Syrians or just plain Arabs. The people on the Red Sea coast were also called Hejazis, and the people inland were named Najdis, after the ruling tribe in each area.

Because of the variety of names, it is difficult, then, to determine just how many people came from the Arabian Peninsula to America. We know that many Arabs came from the Middle East to settle in the United States, often to get better jobs than the ones they had back home. By 1914, over 100,000 Arabs had come to the United States from places in the Middle East.

At first, Muslim Arabs hesitated to come to America for fear they would have a difficult time practicing their religion. They were also afraid that their children would lose their Arab and Islamic identities in the midst of so many non-Muslims. It took time for them to realize that they could build their own mosques and worship as they had done back in Arabia.

Because most of the immigrant Arabs did not know English well and did not like indoor work, the men often became peddlers, or sellers of goods who went from town to town. They would sell any types of goods that were hard to come by outside of the big cities: cloth, sewing needles, pots, pans, dishes, or whatever else people wanted.

American farm families liked to see the peddlers come down the road, since those traveling salespeople could spread the latest news or pass on new information. Many times the farmers would invite the peddlers in for a warm meal and perhaps even a comfortable bed for the night. Little by little, the peddlers began to build up profitable businesses.

Peddlers sometimes settled in small towns and opened stores, selling many of the goods that the farmers and townspeople needed. Middle Eastern people have often been known as good salespersons, and they certainly provided a valuable service to the people of rural America. When they had earned enough money, these Arabs would

This old woodcut shows a peddler selling his goods to a farm family.

send for their families. Then their wives and children would make the long trip from the Middle East to join the head of the family. In time, when there were enough Muslims in a town, they would set up their own place of worship.

Besides becoming shopkeepers, many Arab immigrants became successful farmers. Homesick for the Middle East, they would sometimes name their towns after places in Saudi Arabia. For example, California has a Mecca, and Tennessee, Ohio, and New York each have a Medina.

Some of the earliest immigrants from the Middle East included the four-legged kind. In 1856, a cargo ship delivered thirty-three camels to Texas to help in building up the Southwest. Three Arabs came along to handle the animals, which seemed so suitable for travel in the barren Texas desert.

From 1920 to 1945, very few Arabs came to the United States. Our country had strict immigration laws at that time and did not allow many immigrants into our country. In the 1930s, the terrible Great Depression hit, but the poor economy seemed to hurt the Arab-Americans less than it did other immigrants here. This was because the Arabs had found jobs in grocery stores, restaurants, and peddling. These jobs were less affected by the Depression.

After the Depression, a number of Arabs created successful companies that imported Persian rugs from the Middle East. Even today in large American cities, you can find such businesses which supply beautiful carpets to homes throughout our country.

In 1934, during the Depression, one of the first mosques in the United States was built in Cedar Rapids, Iowa, in the heartland of America. To open the mosque, Saudi Arabia sent over one of its most distinguished religious leaders, Sheik Khalil Al-Rawof. This mosque and ones like it in other areas provided places for Muslims to say their prayers. They also became places for teaching Arabic and for the social get-togethers that Arabs enjoy so much.

The New Wave of Immigrants

After 1945, the United States opened its doors to more and more immigrants. The Arabs who came from the Middle East then were generally more educated than previous settlers. Doctors and other professionals moved to the United States after having attended universities throughout the Arab world.

In the 1960s, more Arabs emigrated from the Middle East to settle in cities such as Detroit, Michigan, and Toledo, Ohio. Many of these Arabs found jobs in the auto factories; of the 85,000 Arabs in Michigan in the early 1960s, 15,000 worked in the auto factories. Today, over 2 million Arabs live in the United States. Perhaps 10 percent of them are Muslims. Most of these Arabs are third- and fourth-generation descendants of Middle Eastern people who arrived here between 1875 and 1948.

One difference that marks Arab immigrants is the close ties that the Arabs kept with their families and friends back home. Many European and Asian immigrants, on the other hand, left their homelands because of religious or political persecution. They left with bitter feelings and intended never to return. This was not the case with most of the Arabs. Many were single men, desiring to earn as much money as possible in America. Sometimes they returned to Saudi Arabia and other Arab countries to set up businesses and build homes. Others would save some money, go back to the Middle East to marry, and bring their new wives to the United States. They kept in touch with their families back home and sent money to relatives. Even today, many Saudis in America frequently make the fourteen-hour plane trip from New York City to Jidda or Riyadh to renew these ties. Their huge phone bills for calls to Saudi Arabia also show how often they communicate with their families there.

Famous Names and Faces

Now that several generations of Arab Americans have settled in the United States, they have begun to make important contributions to America's arts, medicine, sports, and government. The list of distinguished Arab Americans includes former Senator James Abourezk of South Dakota, heart surgeon Dr. Michael De Bakey, and U. S. State Department negotiator Philip Habib. Others include Najeeb Halaby, former president of Pan American World Airways; Casey Kasem, radio and TV announcer; Ralph Nader, active champion of the consumer; Joseph Robbie, late owner of the Miami Dolphins professional football team; John Sununu, former governor of New Hampshire and advisor to President George Bush; and White House reporter Helen Thomas.

While many Arab Americans have entered the mainstream of American life and made important contributions, many others have not completely adopted the American way of life. We often call the United States the great "melting pot" of nations, meaning that it takes in people from many different countries and often makes them similar to each other.

But some immigrants try to enjoy the best of both worlds, the old and the new. They try to hold on to all that was good about their old country, while adopting what is good in the new country. Several thousand Middle Eastern Arabs have done this, for example, in Detroit and Toledo. In these cities, they have formed small Arabic-speaking communities. Here they can keep alive many of the customs from the Arab world and pass on to their children the richness of the Arab way of life. In a sense, they are having the best of both worlds.

Such pockets of people speaking a language other than English, celebrating different types of holidays, eating unusual food, and singing different songs do not in any way hurt the American way of life. On the contrary, they give variety to life in the United States.

Many Arab Muslim communities in the United States have set up mosques in order to worship in the way they were used to back in the Middle East. Unlike many countries in the world, America allows its people to

States, anti-Arab feelings have been strong. Even some of our government officials have been rude to Saudis. When Saudi Arabia and the other OPEC nations raised oil prices, newspapers and magazines often included cartoons of Saudis, showing them as big, fat, unshaven, greedy Arabs interested only in hurting the rest of the world. Such pictures deeply hurt the Saudis and make them wonder where their friends really are. Several Arab-American groups of people are trying to influence newspapers, magazines, and movie companies to stop producing such cartoons.

The Saudis have invested much of their oil profits in the United States, often helping struggling companies or giving loans to individuals. They usually do this without a lot of publicity. They believe that a strong American economy will help keep the world peaceful. For example, the Saudis helped build an underground, energy-efficient elementary school in Reston, Virginia, in 1977. By doing this, they were encouraging the world to conserve energy and use less oil. In the long run, this will benefit everyone, including the Saudis, who can keep their valuable oil that much longer.

Saudi-United States Ties

Each year, the Saudi government sends about 10,000 Saudi students to colleges and universities in the United

When Saudis come to the United States, they often take off their kaffiyehs and wear Western clothes.

States. After they finish their studies, these students will return to Saudi Arabia to become doctors, businessmen, and leaders in their country.

Many princes and leaders in the government have studied at universities in America, especially in southern California, where the warm weather resembles that of Saudi Arabia. They make many friends in the United States. One prince, Sultan Salman Saud, even joined the crew on space shuttle *Discovery* in June 1985, to watch the launch of an Arab communications satellite. Sharing educational and scientific knowledge brings the United States and Saudi Arabia closer all the time.

Among those Saudis who have earned advanced degrees at American universities is Prince Bandar Bin Sultan Bin Abdulaziz. He is the grandson of King Abdulaziz, whom you read about in Chapter 3 of this book.

Prince Bandar earned a master's degree in International Public Policy in 1980 from Johns Hopkins University School of Advanced International Studies in Washington, D.C. In 1983, he became the Ambassador of the Kingdom of Saudi Arabia to the United States of America.

That same year he put into practice what he had learned at Johns Hopkins University as he helped negotiate a cease-fire between the sides fighting each other in the Lebanese civil war. He also regularly attends meetings of the United Nations General Assembly,

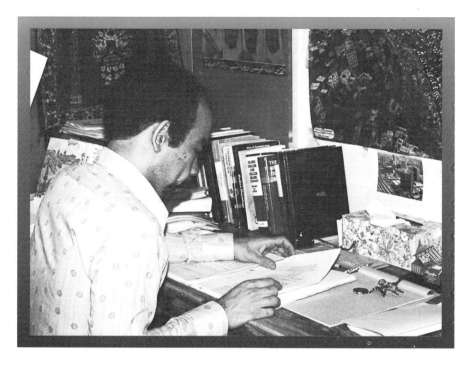

Saudi students often come to American universities to continue their education.

an important group of leaders from around the world who try to maintain or bring about peace in many different countries.

Many Saudi businesspeople have homes in the United States and commute back and forth between Saudi Arabia and this country. About 30,000 Americans work in Saudi Arabia, often taking their families with them. Also, one recent study stated that the jobs of about 1 million American factory workers depend directly on products the United States sells to Saudi Arabia. Our two countries have become very dependent on each other.

*President Bill Clinton meets with King Fahd (right)
during a visit to Saudi Arabia in 1994.*

Because of this closeness, many Americans have taken up the study of the Arabic language. This is especially true of future businesspeople, diplomats, and travelers. Long considered one of the more difficult languages because of its sounds and different letters, Arabic is finding a place in more and more American classrooms.

Several American universities have set up Middle Eastern programs to allow students to study the language, culture, and history of places like Saudi Arabia and to travel to the Middle East to continue their education. With the flow of Saudis to the United States and Americans to Saudi Arabia, the two countries should get to understand and appreciate each other even more than they do now.

As the countries of Saudi Arabia and the United States enter the twenty-first century, they will surely continue to cooperate in many different areas. One recent example shows how that cooperation can work. When Saudi Arabian officials realized that they needed a better system of roads, railroads, airports, and telecommunications, they contacted Americans for help. A large United States aircraft builder, Boeing, joined with Saudia, the national airline of Saudi Arabia, to help establish the Al-Salam Aircraft Company, which is located at King Khalid International Airport in Riyadh.

Workers at the company modify, repair, and manufacture parts for military and civilian airplanes. When the facility opened in 1993, it was the largest of its kind in the entire Middle East and the most modern facility of its kind in the world. Such joint ventures will help Saudi Arabia and its citizens be prepared for entering the twenty-first century and will continue to strengthen relations between Saudis and Americans.

APPENDIX A

Saudi Arabian Consulates in the United States and Canada

The Saudi Arabian consulates in the United States and Canada want to help Americans and Canadians better understand Saudi Arabia. For more information about Saudi Arabia, contact the consulate or embassy nearest you.

United States Consulates and Embassy

Houston, Texas
Consulate General of Saudi Arabia
5718 Westheimer, Suite 1500
Houston, Texas 77057
Phone (713) 785-5577

Los Angeles, California
Consulate General of Saudi Arabia
2045 Sawtelle Boulevard
Los Angeles, California 90025
Phone (310) 479-6000

New York, New York
Consulate General of Saudi Arabia
866 United Nations Plaza, Suite 480
New York, New York 10017
Phone (212) 752-2740

Washington, D. C.
Royal Embassy of Saudi Arabia
601 New Hampshire Avenue, N.W.
Washington, D.C. 20037
Phone (202) 342-3800

Canadian Embassy

Ottawa, Ontario
Royal Embassy of Saudi Arabia
99 Bank Street, Suite 901
Ottawa, Ontario K1P 6B9
Phone (613) 237-4100

APPENDIX B

Arabic Symbols

The Arabic language is a Semitic language. It is related to Hebrew, the only other Semitic language widely spoken today. There are many Arabic dialects, or local ways of speaking, used in countries in the Middle East and northern Africa. A Saudi Arabian speaks a different form of Arabic than does someone from Tunisia or Lebanon. However, formal written Arabic, the language of the Qur'an, is understood throughout the Arabic-speaking world.

Listed below are the symbols of the written Arabic language as well as a guide for pronouncing each symbol. Remember that Arabic is written from right to left, or from the top to the bottom of the page. Also, there are only three vowel sounds in Arabic, which are indicated by small marks written above or below the consonants.

CONSONANTS

Symbol	Sounds Like	Symbol	Sounds Like	Symbol	Sounds Like
ف	f	ب	b	ت	t
د	d	ت	th (*thin*)	ذ	th (*this*)
س	s	ز	z	ش	sh
ج	j	ك	k	م	m
ن	n	ل	l	ر	r
ه	h	و	w	ي	y

The following Arabic symbols do not have equivalents in English, and they are therefore difficult for Westerners to pronounce. The first four symbols are said while spreading the tongue and raising the back of the tongue.

 t   d   s   z

The following two symbols are pronounced with a tightening in the throat.

ح h   ع a

These symbols are produced from the back of the mouth.

خ kh   غ gh

This symbol is pronounced at the back of the throat: ق q.

This symbol sounds like the *u* in butter: أ uh.

VOWELS

These two vowels are written above a consonant.

ـَ a   ـُ u

This vowel is written below a consonant.

ـِ i

Glossary

aba   (AH buh)—a floor-length robe worn by Saudi women

Abdulaziz Al Saud   (ahb dool ah ZEEZ ahl sah OOD) (1880–1953)—the man who created Saudi Arabia and became its king, King Ibn Saud, in 1932

Allah   (AH luh)—the Arabic name for the Supreme Being of Islam

Al Rashid   (ahl ruh SHEED)—the family that fought the Al Saud family for control of Saudi Arabia

Aramco   (uh RAM koh)—the Arabian American Oil Company, the company that produces most of the oil in Saudi Arabia

Bedouin   (BEHD oo ihn)—an Arab who lives in the deserts of Saudi Arabia

calligraphy   (kuh LIHG ruh fee)—the art of fine hand-writing

Fahd   (fahd) (1923–)—the king of Saudi Arabia who began ruling in 1982

Faisal   (FYE sul) (1906?–1975)—the king of Saudi Arabia from 1964 to 1975

kaffiyeh   (kuh FEE yuh)—the long headcovering of the Saudi man that helps keep sand out of his eyes

Hatim Tai   (HAH tihm tay)—the name of a generous, unselfish Arab of legends

Hejaz   (hee JAZ)—the region in northwest Saudi Arabia that includes cities of Mecca and Medina

Hijrah (HIJ ruh)—name of Muhammad's journey from Mecca to Medina in A.D. 622

Id al-Adha (ihd ahl AHD hah)—the Feast of the Sacrifice, a holiday celebrated during pilgrimage time

minaret (mihn uh RET)—a slender tower attached to a mosque from which a man calls Muslims to prayer

Muhammad (moh HAM muhd) (570–632)—an Arab prophet who founded the religion of Islam

Muhammad ibn Abd al Wahhab (moh HAM muhd ihb-un ahbd ahl wah HAHB) (1703–1792)—a Muslim religious reformer

mosque (mahsk)—an Islamic place of public religious worship

Mehemet Ali (meh MET ah lee) (1769–1849)—an Egyptian general who fought against the Arabs in the Arabian Peninsula

Nabateans (nab uh TEE unz)—people who lived in the northwestern corner of the Arabian Peninsula many years ago

OPEC (OH pek)—the Organization of Petroleum Exporting Countries, which countries depend on oil exports for income

Qur'an (kuh RAN)—the sacred book of the Muslims

Ramadan (ram uh DAHN)—the ninth month in the Islamic year, in which Muslim adults eat and drink nothing during the daylight hours

riyal (ree YAHL)—the unit of money used in Saudi Arabia

Rub Al Khali   (roob   ahl   KAH lee)—the desert in the
    southern part of Saudi Arabia

Saud   (sah OOD) (1902–1969)—Saudi Arabia's second
    king, who ruled from 1953 to 1964

thawb   (thawb)—the long one-piece garment that Saudi
    men wear

SELECTED BIBLIOGRAPHY

Al-Sweel, Abdulaziz I., editor. *Saudi Arabia: A Kingdom in Transition*. Beltsville, MD: Amana Publications, 1993.

Farsy, Fouad. *Modernity and Tradition: The Saudi Equation*. London: Kegan Paul International, 1990.

Hirashima, Hussein Yoshio. *The Road to Holy Mecca*. New York: Kodansha International, 1972.

Leipold, L. E. *Come Along to Saudi Arabia*. Minneapolis: T. S. Denison & Co., 1974.

Lipsky, George A., and others. *Saudi Arabia*. New Haven, CT: Human Relations Area File Press, 1959.

Saudi Arabia in Pictures. New York: Sterling Publishing Co., 1978 (revised edition).

Wood, Geraldine. *Saudi Arabia*. New York: Franklin Watts, 1978.

Yamani, Mohammad Abdo. *A Boy From Mecca*. London: Cassell, 1981.

INDEX

Abdulaziz Al Saud, 33, 38. *See also* Ibn Saud (king)
Abourezk, James, 109
Ad Dammam, 16, 17, 19
Al Rashid family, 33
Al Saud family, 19, 33–34, 38, 41
Al Wahhab, Muhammad ibn Abd, 37–38
Al-Rawof, Khalil, 107
Al-Salam Aircraft Company, 117
Ali, Mehemet, 38
Arab-Israeli wars, 44, 111
Arabian Peninsula, 4, 7, 20, 33, 34, 35, 37, 38, 104
Arabic language, 4, 49–51, 116, 120–121
Aramco (Arabian American Oil Company), 17, 40, 43, 46
Ardah, 65

Bandar (prince), 114–115
Bedouins, 28–32, 83, 95, 96
Bush, George, 47

calendar, 25, 62
calligraphy, 52
clothing, 31, 32, 74, 75, 77–79, 111

De Bakey, Michael, 109
desalination, 13
deserts, 10, 12–14, 17, 18, 28–32, 54, *89*, 100
Dhahran, 17

economy, 47–48: products, 4, 25–26. *See also* oil
education, 83–91: disabled students, 88; elementary school, 86; high school, 87; subjects studied, 85, 86, 87; universities, 75, 76, 86, 88, 90, 113, 114; vocational schools, 86
Empty Quarter. *See Rub al Khali*

Fahd (king), 46, 47, 72, 116

Faisal (king), 42–43, 44
food, 59, 61, 62–63, 65–70: taboulleh, 69–70

gestures, 52–53

Habib, Philip, 109
Halaby, Najeeb, 109
Hatim Tai, 54, 56, 58
Hejaz Railway, 38
Hijrah, 25
holidays, 5, 59–65: Id al-Adha, 5, 59–61; Id al-Fitr, 5, 62–63; king's holidays, 64–65; National Day, 5, 63; prayer days, 64

Ibn Saud (king), 40, 41, 42, 104. *See also* Abdulaziz Al Saud
Iraq, 9, 20, 47
Islam, 5, 14, 19, 20, 21–25, 31, 35, 37–38, 40, 43, 49, 52, 71, 75
Israel, 43, 44, 46

Jidda, *15*, 16, 17, 19, 20, 22, 27, 79, 100

Kasem, Casey, 109
Khalid (king), 46
King Khalid International Airport, 18, 117
Koran. *See* Qur'an
Kuwait, 9, 20, 33, 47

Lawrence of Arabia. *See* Lawrence, T.E.
Lawrence, T.E., 38, *39*

Madinah. *See* Medina
Makkah. *See* Mecca
marriage, 75–77
Mecca, 5, 14, 15, 16, 21, 24, 37, 38, 48, 59, *60*, 61
Medina, 5, 14, 15, 16, 25, 37, 38, 48, 59, 60, 61

mosques, 21, 22, 23, 85, 105, 107, 110
Muhammad, 5, 14, 24, 25, 35, 49, 90
Muslims, 14, 15, 19, 20, 24, 43, 49, 59, 62, 75, 105, 106, 107, 108

Nabateans, 34–35, 36
Nader, Ralph, 109
names, 71–74

oil, 7, 9, 14, 16–17, 20, 25–26, 40–41, 43, 46–48, 86, 111, 113
OPEC (Organization of Petroleum Exporting Countries), 17, 46, 113

Palestinians, 43, 44
Persian Gulf, 9, 16
Persian Gulf War, 20, 47
proverbs, 26, 49, 71, 91

Qur'an, 24, 49, *52*, 68, 83, 85, 87

Ramadan, 5, 62–63
Red Sea, 9, 16, 35, 97, 100
Riyadh, 4, 17–19, 20, 22, 27, 33, 40, 46, 79, 92, 95, 117
Robbie, Joseph, 109
Rub al Khali, 10

Saud (king), 41, 42
Saud, Salman, 114
Saudi Arabia: city life in, 79–82; climate of, 9; currency of, 4; flag of, 5, 24, 59, 65; geography of, 4, 7–14; government of, 4, 19, 25; home page of, 5; immigrants to U.S. from, 104–117; location of, 4, 7; population of, 4, 18; relations with U.S., 44, 46–47, 104–117
Schwarzkopf, Norman, 47
sex roles, 22, 86, 88, 98: men, 65, 66, 71–72, 75, 76, 77–79; women, 22, 30–31, 65–66, 74–77
sports, 92–103: camel races, 92–95; desert sports, 100–103; falconry, 95–96; horse races, 95; hunting, 95–97; soccer, 97; water sports, 98–100
stories, 54–58
Suez Canal, 16

Sununu, John, 109
sword dance. *See* Ardah

Thomas, Helen, 109
Turks, 37, 38, 104

water, 9, 12–14, 16, 28, 30, 35
wildlife, *10*, *11*, 31, 96–97, 100, *101*
workers, 17, 27

ABOUT THE AUTHOR

Kevin McCarthy has experienced life in several Middle Eastern countries, first as a Peace Corps volunteer in Turkey and then as a college professor in Lebanon and in Saudi Arabia, the subject of his first children's book.

Mr. McCarthy feels that many books about Saudi Arabia give a negative or incomplete picture of the country. In *Saudi Arabia: A Desert Kingdom*, he has tried to tell the whole story and show both the good and bad points of these Middle Eastern people.

Among Mr. McCarthy's published works are an English textbook as well as two textbooks that are now being used in Saudi universities. He has also had ten other books published on a variety of subjects such as lighthouses, shipwrecks, pirates, football, baseball, and literature. While living in Saudi Arabia, he hosted three radio programs a week on national Saudi radio. He is currently a professor of English and linguistics at the University of Florida, Gainesville. Mr. McCarthy lives in Florida with his family.